My Life in San Juan Pueblo

My Life in San Juan Pueblo

STORIES OF ESTHER MARTINEZ

Edited by Sue-Ellen Jacobs and Josephine Binford
with M. Ellien Carroll, Henrietta M. Smith,
and Tilar Mazzeo

Foreword by Tessie Naranjo

University of Illinois Press
Urbana, Chicago, and Springfield

∞ This book is printed on acid-free paper.

Library of Congress Cataloging-in-Publication Data
My life in San Juan Pueblo : stories of Esther Martinez / edited by
Sue-Ellen Jacobs and Josephine Binford, with M. Ellien Carroll,
Henrietta M. Smith, and Tilar Mazzeo ; foreword by Tessie Naranjo.
        p.   cm.
Includes bibliographical references (p.) and index.
ISBN 978-0-252-02889-2 (cl. : alk. paper)
ISBN 978-0-252-07158-4 (pbk. : alk. paper)
1. Tewa Indians—Folklore.
2. Tales—New Mexico—San Juan Pueblo.
3. P'oe Tsǫ́wą́ʔ.
4. Storytellers—New Mexico—San Juan Pueblo—Biography.
5. Tewa Indians—Biography.
I. Jacobs, Sue-Ellen. II. Binford, Josephine. III. Title.
E99.T35P64   2004
398.2'089'9749—dc21   2003007104

*This book is dedicated to
my children,
my grandchildren,
my great-grandchildren,
and my great-great-grandchildren.*

CONTENTS

PART 2: THEHTÁY'S STORIES—AS I TELL THEM

Photographs follow page 142

FOREWORD

Tessie Naranjo

I was honored when Kóʔôe Esther asked me to write the foreword for her book. Kóʔôe and I do not come from the same community. Our communities are six miles apart, but we share our Tewa language, our values, and much of our worldview. The stories told by Kóʔôe Esther have as much meaning and applicability here in Santa Clara Pueblo as they do in her home in San Juan Pueblo. Kóʔôe Esther is a story-teller, and that is a position, a craft, that is held in high regard among all Tewa community people who remember those times when our elders sat down with us to tell stories. We call her Kóʔôe or Aunt because it is a title of respect and affection. Our stories are our literature. The stories convey our reality, our hopes, and our dreams.

The stories told by our elders gave us lessons in community standards and values, our place within the community, descriptions of proper and improper behavior, and our relationships with other people. Storytelling connects us to our past. It gives us the basis from which to grow and become productive members of our society. In the story of "Little Black Ants and Old Man Coyote," Coyote's haste causes him to collect sand and gravel with his wheat. He also sings the ants' grinding song, which he thinks is his song to use. He makes a fool of himself in these ways, and we are reminded of the humor in his foolishness throughout the story. We are reminded to share several times in the same story, when the ants allow Coyote to join them in the wheat grinding and again when Coyote offers to share his flour with the ants. We are also reminded of the importance of work to prevent hunger. Work is a basic value, and the story reminds us of its importance. Kóʔôe Esther was born at a time when storytelling was one of the only available means to pass on identity, social expectations, and cosmology. In many ways, and by our choice, this is still the way it is. We maintain oral traditions in the most important areas of our lives. Kó'ôe's storytelling is part of a tradition that goes to our beginnings and creates our future.

We come from a tradition that values the music of language, its poetry, and its ability to conjure images. There is a love for the sound of the language, a love for the beauty of a phrase. One of the beauties of our language is its tonality. Tewa is a tonal language, and the words sing to you as they are spoken. The language is also full of words that represent things by their sounds. For instance, the Tewa word for bird is tsídé. Our word for wind is wąą. We also tend to be indirect in speech. We will often describe and discuss events metaphorically. A few days before writing this, I was driving with my mother. She looked up and said, in Tewa, "The clouds are hatching eggs." I looked up at the burgeoning clouds and knew without thinking about it that she meant that it was likely to rain. In a world like this, a storyteller is a person who uses all the tonality and imagery of the language to carry the meaning and mood of the tale that they are telling. This carries into Kó'ôe's English versions of her stories. She uses a different language structure than a native English-speaker would be likely to select. That structure reinforces the power of the stories. Part of the joy of seeing Kó'ôe Esther's stories preserved is a joy of knowing that our love of language is being honored.

Kó'ôe, in her introduction, talks about her "life's path," or in Tewa terms her p'ôe'ą́ą̈. The community belief system says that we are to seek life with care and consideration for it wherever it is found—and life is found everywhere. Each of us finds our life's path, our p'ôe'ą́ą̈. Our path is how we make our way through all of life. It is our duty to live according to its dictates. Kó'ôe Esther's stories often illustrate, sometimes by examples from her experiences, the proper ways for us to walk through life. In her story "My Stuffed Squirrel," Kó'ôe receives the gift of a stuffed squirrel made by her grandfather. She did not have the stuffed squirrel long before it was taken by her puppy and lost forever. Kó'ôe knew that she could not ask her grandfather to make her another stuffed squirrel. Kó'ôe was supposed to take care of that one, but when it was lost she knew that she could not ask for another.

This experience was one that shaped her character. She knew that asking for another meant that she had not cared for the first. The lesson in the story is that in our life's path one must walk and behave carefully. Kóʔôe, when recounting her experience in the loss of her stuffed squirrel, shows us that lack of proper care can lead to loss. If unchecked, the loss can be serious.

Kóʔôe uses her storytelling as a means to educate, to entertain, and to delight and give life to those who listen. Some years ago, pottery figurines depicting storytellers, covered and surrounded by listening clay children, became popular. These figures have captured people's imaginations. Kóʔôe Esther is a living storyteller, telling her stories to all who can hear them. Here, in her own words, is the person the potters who make these images have been depicting in clay.

ACKNOWLEDGMENTS

I want to thank all of the people who have helped me put this book together, starting with my daughter Ahkon Póvi (Josephine Binford). She has helped me write and edit the Introduction and has been deeply involved in the reorganization of the book so that it reflects my life and my grandfather's stories. She moved back to San Juan Pueblo in 1997 to help me when my health was a little off. Next, I want to thank M. Ellien Carroll for giving me the opportunity to become a storyteller outside my community. When I had retired for the third time I began to miss the children at the Day School so much. Ellien came into my life at just the right moment, making it possible for me to tell stories to children and grownups throughout New Mexico and elsewhere. Her friendship remains very important to me, even though she has had to move to California. We stay in touch by telephone now. Thanks also go to Henrietta Smith for her friendship, her hospitality and sharing of stories during my visit to her community in Florida, and her hard work of putting the stories in order in the first place. The University of Washington Department of Women Studies gets my thanks for helping with transcription of my storytelling tapes and production of the many drafts and the final version of the manuscript for this book. Sue-Ellen Jacobs has been the central person responsible for seeing the book through all stages of production. To Tessie Naranjo, my Santa Clara Pueblo friend and colleague in Pueblo studies, special thanks for her suggestions and willingness to help with revisions. I am also grateful to Tessie for writing the Foreword. Tessie joined my daughter, Josephine Binford, and Sue-Ellen Jacobs in the proofreading. Tessie and Sue-Ellen also composed the index, and under great pressure— the first time to do this kind of a job, and with deadlines facing them on several projects. Thanks to both of them. I have known Tessie for many years and have enjoyed our collaborative work on many projects. Thank you also to Margaret MacDonald for her critical and supportive review of this book. Margaret's suggested changes have helped us keep the storytelling mission of the book intact. I thank Randy Speirs for giving me the chance to learn how to write the stories in my language and for his long-standing friendship and the many opportunities to work together to keep my language alive. Most of all, I thank my elders, especially my grandfather and my grandmother, for the stories they gave me as I was growing up, and my children, grandchildren, and great-grandchildren for listening to the many times I have told these stories (and others) to them.

—Blue Water

We thank Siri Tuttle for her linguistic assistance in transcribing and editing all of the Tewa materials and for production of the song lyrics and scores with the support of the Center for Advanced Research Technology in the Arts and Humanities (CARTAH) at the University of Washington. She and Ewa Trebacz, a Ph.D. student in the University of Washington Department of Music, used FINALE to generate the music and lyrics in the stories. We thank Ewa for taking time from her studies to help us at a critical moment. A special thank you to Chrystos, who gave up two days of her own creative work to proofread and edit manuscript version number nineteen. Thanks to Mark Haslam and Stacy Waters of CARTAH for technical laboratory assistance with FINALE. We also extend thanks to Greg R. Sadowski for his excellent technical editing and data entry for manuscript version number nineteen, to Jason Cromwell for his help with reviewing the copyediting, and to Adrianna Jones, one of Esther Martinez's six granddaughters, for providing us with a fresh pair of eyes and serious critical revisions during the final days of copyediting. All of us wish to signal special appreciation to Elizabeth Dulany, associate director, retired, Theresa L. Sears, managing editor, Mary Giles, associate editor, and Willis Regier, director, of the University of Illinois Press, who kept faith in this book and worked with us through some difficult times.

—Sue-Ellen Jacobs
Esther Martinez
Josephine Binford

My Life in San Juan Pueblo

Figure 1. Esther Martinez at San Juan Pueblo Lakes, 1994. (Sue-Ellen Jacobs)

I was born in 1912, the year the *Titanic* sank and the year New Mexico became a state. I was born in Utah because my parents were there for my dad to work in the mines in Ute Agency country in southwestern Colorado. When I was a baby they moved to Colorado. My dad was a jack of all trades. He had worked in the coal, silver, and gold mines. Then he worked as a janitor, milkman, gardener, and night watchman in the U.S. Bureau of Indian Affairs boarding school for Indian children. When I was about four years old I wanted to go to school, so I asked my mother if I could go. So after asking my father for permission, he let me follow him around while he was doing his work at the boarding school.

I lived in Colorado with my mother and father until I was around the age of five. I had learned to speak my Tewa language while living with them. They always spoke to us in our language. Then one day my grandparents from New Mexico came to visit, and when they were returning back to the village I tagged along. After that I stayed with my grandparents, and I was their tail, an endless tag-along. So I was raised in San Juan Pueblo, New Mexico, known as Ohkay Owînge in Tewa, my Native language. San Juan Pueblo is located near where the Rio Chama and the Rio Grande rivers come together. It is one of the Eight Northern Indian Pueblos and one of the six Tewa-speaking tribes.

When I first left Ute country and arrived in Tewa country I missed my little brother, who was my playmate. Then one day my grandparents were going back to visit my folks in Colorado, and on this trip I "tricked" my little brother to return back with me to New Mexico. After that we were inseparable. My parents were blessed with four girls and four boys. I was third in line.

My brother and I, the one I had tricked to come back with me to New Mexico, were both raised by our grandparents. We had a very happy childhood. We were lucky to be raised by two loving and caring grandparents. Growing up in the Indian village was fun because the whole village was there for you. A child was never alone even if he or she was playing in the plaza; there was always a grown-up nearby to guide us in our pathway to adulthood. I was raised during the time when there were no McDonalds, no Kentucky Fried Chicken, no motels, no television or telephones. As a child, our television was our inquisitive, creative imagination, and our telephone was knocking on the wall to your neighbor's wall since we shared one wall.

You see, our homes were all made of adobes [mud bricks] built in rows, and most were one level but some had one additional room built on top. These top rooms were generally used in the summertime because they were cooler. Every door had a family living there. Our houses were all together. There is a family here, a family there, and maybe this family and this family share a wall. So this wall is one that belongs to the two families. If somebody wants to buy this house, or if this family wants to sell or trade with another one on the other side, and if somebody else comes to live here, this person and this person own that wall. My grandmother lived right next to her younger sister. When she wanted her younger sister to come over and have coffee with her, or when she has something to offer her, she just knocked on the wall. My aunt would come and say, "What do you want?" My grandmother would say, "I want to have some coffee with you." So they would sit and have coffee and talk. And that was nice. Another time my aunt would knock on the wall and my grandmother would go over there. So you see we had our own special telephones. They were cheaper and we always knew who was calling, so who needed caller ID? Anyway, ours were more fun to use.

I was born when Mother Nature was very respected, when the water was pure and good to drink. When I was growing up, you see a stream flowing, you can just get down on your tummy and take a drink. Nowadays we cannot because upstream there may be a dead animal, or you may see a dirty Pamper floating in the stream. In my days people took care of Mother Nature.

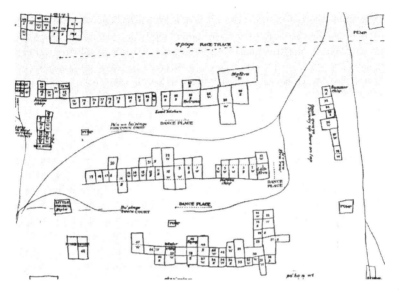

Figure 2. "Houses of San Juan Pueblo, Drawn by a Townswoman," map 2. Each internal line represents the common wall between adjoining houses. (Elsie Clews Parsons; courtesy of the American Anthropological Association, from Memoir 36, 1929)

Growing up in my village, in my grandparents' house, things were a lot different. We did not have furniture—no tables, no chairs, and no lamps. We had a bedroll—a mattress we would pull out at night and roll up in the morning—and it was placed against the wall. That was used for sitting, that was our chair. Our rooms were small, but we had plenty of room to get around. I suppose we were poor in that way, with material things. But I didn't miss any of it because I had all the elders in the village who were always handy. I never worried about who was going to comfort me if anybody made me cry or if I needed any other care. If I got in trouble they corrected me right on the spot. I never got spanked. I was taught Indian values in the village. I was taught to respect my elders, to respect my friends, and to respect myself. It was nice. It was a nice way to learn because people cared.

Children are my favorite [audience]; whenever I have children I enjoy telling stories because their imaginations are fresh yet. As I told a group, an audience that I had of elderly people, and they came from all walks of life, and I told them, "Turn your buttons back and be a child. Tonight you will hear children's stories." That was the day Ellien [Carroll] and I were invited to the New Mexico Arts Commission's Governor's Award for Excellence and Achievement in the Arts presentation. This was the first time a Native American storyteller ever was given this recognition. They have been given awards for their paintings, and the artists were telling where they have been with their paintings. I told them I never went anywhere with my "paintings," my paintings are all done in the minds of my audience, my artwork lives in the heart of people.

A question I am often asked is, When did you first start storytelling? Well, when I was in school I did not know how to read yet. But I had a Dick and Jane book, and I brought it home one time. My grandmother was sitting there, looking at the pictures, and then she said, "Come here. Tell me what it says here." She was pointing at the lines, she thought I was able to read. Since she thought that I was able to, I did. I looked at the picture and just imagined in my own head what they were doing. So I pointed to the lines and pretended that I was reading from them, and I told her what they were doing there. I guess she liked the story. She just sat there and looked at the pictures; then the next day or three days later she had the book again, I was there. She said, "Come here and read the story to me again. What are they doing here?" So I looked at them, and then I started pointing and gave her another story, a different story. I think that was the beginning of my storytelling.

In my village we had many, many storytellers, not just my grandparents. Storytelling done by my grandparents was special to me because I got to sit on their laps; it was private and done especially for us (my brother and me). In those days the doors were not locked. Storytellers would let us know they were not home by placing a medium-sized rock in front of the screen door.

At storytelling there was always a basket of piñons in the middle of the floor. We all sat on floors, and kids helped by cracking the piñons. At home, my grandparents would limit my brother and me to one handful of piñons. But when we were visiting other storytellers' homes we always got a pocketful. (Piñons are little shelled pine seeds about the size of a sunflower seed. When roasted they are delicious). Anyway, storytelling was done mainly in the wintertime, not summer. It was done in the wintertime because it shortened the evenings, the long winter nights. And it was the time when the last snake had crawled in, the bear and other animals had gone hibernating, and we have heard the last of the thunders. At storytelling, children's stories were told first. Stories were told to teach us tips for survival [see the "Hungry Coyote and Rabbit" story] and for socialization in the community. They were fun. Our whole life is about storytelling.

Sometimes when I am out storytelling, audience members are invited to ask questions after the story is told. For example, Ellien recorded the following questions and my responses:

Could we hear the Tewa language and maybe do the counting?
You are going to count with me to ten. Our numbers: number five has a funny sound, so you be aware of that. It has a popping beginning sound. And the number eight has that sound that comes from the throat. Number six sounds almost like your six in English; number ten sounds almost like your ten in English. Number five is the only one you have to watch for because that has p'. Okay. Wí⁷ [one]. Wíyeh [two]. Poeyeh [three]. Yôenu [four]. P'ą́ąnú [five]. Sí [six]. Tséh [seven]. Khâaveh [eight]. Whą́ą́nu [nine]. Tą̌ [ten].

How do you say twenty, thirty?
From ten to eleven is ten plus one; ten plus two, for twelve; up to nineteen. When you count to twenty, we say ten times two, and then thirty is ten times three, so it is a times table all the way up to a thousand. When I worked in the bilingual classroom, I would tell the children, "You already know your times tables, because you have it in the Native language." If it is thirty-five, you would say three times ten plus five.[1]

---

1. "Tewa Language: Counting." Tape 4, told at STORYFIESTA™, 1997. Recorded by M. Ellien Carroll. Transcribed and edited by Tilar Mazzeo; edited by Sue-Ellen Jacobs, Henrietta M. Smith, and M. Ellien Carroll.

I don't know who ever thought of the language, but it always amazed me when I was teaching. There are so many ways that they say things. And the numbers are just times whatever the number it is, ten times five plus nine for fifty-nine or whatever. It is interesting. We are losing the language fast, and we are trying to revive it.

For more examples of audience questions and my answers, see Appendix 1, "Examples of Audience's Questions and My Answers."

I have met many, many wonderful people throughout my p'ôe'ą̈ą̈ [life journey], in my adventures as a mother, a grandmother, a storyteller, a bilingual teacher, a consultant, a tribal member, and an elder. All these individuals have had a great impact on my life in one way or another. Traveling my p'ôe'ą̈ą̈ was not easy; seeking new adventures was. The child in me wanting the answers to the why, the where, and the how come has made my life of seeking and searching for answers fun and entertaining. So now I will tell you about a few of the individuals I have met, how they influenced the direction of my life and helped weave my character and made me the individual that I have become.

The word *pehtsiye* is "storytelling" in our language. It is an oral tradition and involves the sharing of knowledge and entertainment from one generation to the next. *Pehtsiye-ây: Little Tewa Stories,* [the book] that Ellien found [containing] my grandfather's stories were written down in the Tewa language and then in English. Randy Speirs did that with me. All of my grandfather's stories were in my computer, my head, until one day [in the 1960s] I met a linguist named Randy Speirs. He was in the process of writing our language in a contemporary linguistic form. Later, he asked me if I wanted to learn to read and write my language. I said yes. I was around fifty-four years old. Learning the little sounds and learning to read and write my language was very hard. I was a fluent speaker of Tewa, but writing Tewa and listening to the detail of the sounds was a challenge. I practiced and I practiced my sounds and writing. Finally I learned. Of course the lessons I got in linguistics at the University of North Dakota and again at Saint John's College in Santa Fe helped me learn how to be able to write Tewa, and that made it possible for me to become a bilingual teacher at the San Juan Pueblo Day School in 1966, along with a great staff that included Peter Povijual, Artie Ortiz, Frances Harney, Gertrude Calvert, Marie J. Abeyta, and Laura Calvert. At the Day School, we worked with Randy on writing the San Juan Pueblo Tewa Dictionary, the curriculum guides, and the little storybooks. In the beginning Randy helped me get my grandfather's stories written in Tewa and also some are written in English. Somehow one of our little books landed in a used book store, which later got me in touch with Ellien Carroll.

The next person I met who is part of putting this book together was Sue-Ellen Jacobs. We met in 1972 through our mutual friend, Bill Leap, a linguist at American University in Washington, D.C. Bill had been visiting with me to learn about Tewa-English. This was when he was studying "Indian English." Sue-Ellen was in New Mexico visiting with friends and recording stories from several of the elders. She and I talked about how we were working on stories and agreed to share whatever we got that would be of interest to our respective projects. Over the years we continued in casual contact, but in 1994 we came together to begin transcribing the tapes of stories she had collected from the elders. This led to our work together on the Tewa Language Project that lasted six years. With the help of lots of community people and students and staff at the University of Washington, we produced a set of teaching and research CD-ROMs for my people and presented them to the tribe in December 2000.

I met Ellien Carroll, through Randy Speirs, in 1986. I had written some little storybooks for the children at the Day School. Somehow one of the books got to a used book store. My friend Ellien always looks for books that are discarded. She never looks at the ones that are on the shelves. She looks through the basket where the books that are not wanted anymore are thrown, and she always finds a treasure there. And that is what she was doing one day. I don't remember what bookstore she had gone to, but she had found a little book, I think it was the first one that I had written for the children. She needed a little verse or just a sentence that she wanted to include in her magazine. She asked Randy, since Randy had his name and phone number written on there too. So Randy told her, "You have to ask Esther since she is the one who writes the little books." So that is how we met. Randy told her how to contact me. So she did. It was close to our Feast Day, so I invited her to come and join us for the San Juan Feast Day. I think we just stuck together like glue after that. I went to the storytelling they had in Albuquerque. It was during the balloon festival, and they had a tent built for storytellers, and that was where I first told my stories away from San Juan. Whenever they asked for a storyteller, Ellien would come and get me, and we would go. We traveled all over: twenty-two libraries in New Mexico; storytelling conferences in Colorado, California, Nebraska, New Mexico, and Florida; special occasions such as when the Hells Angels escorted Ellien and me on their motorcycles when I was to tell stories at the New Mexico State Fair; to the University of Washington to tell stories to students and Native communities' members; and to students in schools throughout New Mexico and in Florida and many more places. Ellien would sometimes record my stories, and that is how we happened to have the stories in this book.

I met Henrietta Smith in Albuquerque at a STORYFIESTA™ gathering hosted by Storytellers International™. There were a bunch of storytellers there. We took turns telling stories in the evening when we gathered. Because she was so far away from home, when Ellien and I went out storytelling in New Mexico we always had Henrietta along with us until she went back to Florida. She is African American from Florida and tells stories from African American and southern U.S. cultural traditions.

In May of 1992 I had the pleasure of visiting Henrietta at her home in Florida. I will always remember all the grapefruits on the ground and on the trees in her backyard! I went there to meet her family, and her friends, and to tell stories at the Annual Broward County Children's Reading Festival. She works in a library. She took us over there to visit her in the library, and later I told the story of the Deer Dance at the reading festival.

I had three girls and seven boys. Now, I have nineteen grandchildren, twenty-two great-grandchildren, and five great-great grandchildren. Most of them still live around San Juan Pueblo. My house is always noisy, and it is like Grand Central Station. I enjoy our times together, sometimes I forget who is who. At my age, ninety, it is okay. Anyway my eyesight is not as good, now I have someone read to me.

Even my ears don't hear as good, and my handwriting is on a slant instead of a straight line. I suppose that is what happens when you become an elder. You walk slower because of arthritis, and you ask people to speak louder. Sometimes I don't feel old. It's just that my body cannot keep up physically with my brain. Now I find myself taking catnaps wherever I go. Everyone should take a catnap once in awhile.

I suppose now you are all wondering how I manage my daily chores. Well, I have help. I have two sons, one grandson, and one daughter living with me. They all see to my needs, each in their own unique way. Sometimes the boys will take me fishing at the Rio Grande River. It is funny, but everytime we go fishing I catch more fish than they do. They are always being teased. I enjoy those moments. Fishing and being outdoors, gardening, are two of my favorite hobbies. My daughter tends to all of my daily needs, braids my long hair, and makes sure that I am clean and neat. Sometimes she is overprotecting, but I know it is for my best interest. She says I am at high risk for falls. I suppose that is the nurse in her coming out. Sometimes my older daughter will take me to her house for coffee and to have a piece of fresh-baked pie. Then, I have one daughter living in Navajo country in northern New Mexico. She will come get me to visit for the weekend. While visiting we will feast on mutton stew. We also go to the flea market in Farmington. And the grandkids are always visiting. So you see I am never alone.

Back at the village, I get a noon meal delivered by the Senior Program because it is now hard for me to get up into and down from the van to go to our senior center. My knees now have snaps, crackles and pops because of arthritis.

My daughter who lives with me also writes my letters. I tell her what to write, and she writes it then reads it back to me. Sometimes when my ears are being naughty she takes the telephone calls and tells me what people are saying. I don't bang on walls anymore.

People still come to my house wanting help with information for their college paper or wanting a storyteller. Young folks from the village, who were once my students in bilingual classes, will now stop by for advice on traditional values or wanting me to give Indian names to their kids or grandkids. One young grandmother from a neighboring Tewa village even came to ask me for permission to name her granddaughter after me. So now we have another little Blue Water. I am honored.

Others may stop by for help in knowing about or identifying traditional herbs or for help or advice in planting or gardening. As a young woman I had worked in Los Alamos as a housekeeper. Now I am asked questions about how it was in Los Alamos in the early days during the time of World War II. Some folks that have interviewed me came from far away, as far as Germany, Japan, and even a princess from Spain. Next week, on February 28, 2002, I will be going to Springer and Raton, New Mexico, again to tell stories to children at their schools for the Dr. Suess Read across America Week. I am very excited about going. This is my pʼôeʔą́ą̈. I am still traveling. As you can see I am still busy.

PART 1

Autobiographical Stories

Who Are My People and How Do We Live?

The River at San Juan Pueblo

The settlement was in a little area. Do you see that mound around there? That used to be an Indian settlement. Then the people moved across the river and these people came, and that is their place. They settled there.

Our river was full of precious things in those days. We went there because we got our drinking water from the river. No matter where you were, you could always get down on your tummy and take a drink. It is not so anymore. People trash up the place. They do not seem to know how to take care of Mother Earth anymore. But when I was growing up as a little girl, the water was safe to drink. Even the people who lived up above, that way, could get the water. It was the water for drinking, and washing, and bathing, for everything we do without running water inside. So they took good care of it. They did not throw in dead animals or dirty diapers and stuff like that which you see in the river now. You cannot use it for drinking any more.

I used to always come and get water from the river to wash my hair. It was like soft water, the river water.

And the water in the river, I said, is precious to all the Native people because it means raising a crop. You have a seed in the ground that has to be watered. So there is an irrigation ditch that flows right here, almost up between the trees and comes out just below there. There is another river that comes down on that side, called the Chama River. That flows down back, because it is more downhill. So that is full of water when the snow melts.

"The River at San Juan Pueblo." Tape 5, told at the San Juan Pueblo Church for visiting students from Los Alamos High School, March 1998. Recorded by M. Ellien Carroll. Transcribed and edited by Tilar Mazzeo; edited by Sue-Ellen Jacobs, Henrietta M. Smith, and M. Ellien Carroll.

Figure 3. The confluence of the Rio Grande and Chama rivers, (lower left) with the San Pedro across (lower right), 1973. (John D. Jacobs)

There were many springs when the water gets filled up and fishes get washed up on the banks. There was one time when I remember— I was a little girl, I guess—I remember there was a man coming, and he saw the river had overflowed. And there were a lot of fish on the bank. And another old man who wore the Native clothing, and he is the town crier. He wore leggings with a belt. And then he wore a g-string. All men wore g-strings, covered with a blanket or light cloth. But he got all excited when he came and saw [all the] fishes.

All the fishes that they take are not for just one family. They pass them out to whoever is around and cannot come to the river to get so many fish flapping around on the banks. He went in the water and got all the paa [fish]. So he went home with one paa, and everybody had fish to eat.

And then there was too many, but my people did not waste their food. If they had more than they could eat, they would give to the neighbor, and if the neighbor already had more than they could eat they would build a fire outside, in those dome ovens. They build a fire in those ovens, and then they take the fish from there, and they hang them

Figure 4. San Juan Pueblo women winnowing wheat, 1935, by T. Harmon Parkhurst. (Courtesy Museum of New Mexico, Neg. No. 55192)

up. The whole village shares with others, and I do not know, I guess when they get hungry they like to eat. I remember my grandmother used to make fish stew with a little red chili added to it, and I suppose that was a good dish for them because they are always making it.

And the river is also used when people plow and plant wheat in their fields. They will have enough wheat to grind into the flour. The wheat has to be washed in the river, and you do not need strong running water to do that, you need just a little stream. Or at the edge of the bank, where the ground is flat, you can just put down a canvas with your wet things on the canvas to dry. You do not winnow it till it gets dry-dry. Only so, when you bite into it, it will just barely crack. [Next you winnow the wheat to get rid of the chaff.] Then it is ready to go to the mill for flour. And so we use the river like that.

And then, much earlier, the young boys who were able to stay up nights would make little fish traps with a willow that is growing around in the area. They make their fish traps about two feet long—wide on top and v-shaped on the bottom, so that it opens just one way. From the inside the fish cannot get out, because the door closed, and when the fish want to get out the opening there, they are trapped.

Summer and Winter Wells

Everywhere my people went, they always dug two wells, one on the south side for the Summer people, and one on the north side for the Winter people. My grandmother is a Winter woman, but to reach the spring that belongs to the Winter people, she had to come up a higher hill, and for the Summer people the hill was sort of flat, so it was easier for her to get water there. So it did not matter if you were a Winter person and got water in the Summer well. It was okay.

"Summer and Winter Wells." Tape 4, told at STORYFIESTA™, Albuquerque, 1997. Recorded by M. Ellien Caroll. Transcribed and edited by Tilar Mazzeo; edited by Sue-Ellen Jacobs, Henrietta M. Smith, and M. Ellien Carroll.

San Juan Pueblo: Winter and Summer Chiefs

Remember that we have a Winter Chief and a Summer Chief. These days, the Summer Chief is gone [dead] and the Winter Chief is also gone [dead]. He went before the Summer Chief, so we do not have the Summer Chief, but we still have societies. We had different societies. We have the Medicine Society, the Clown Society. . . . But mostly the clowns and the medicine; that is all we have now, because, as I said, all the new ones who want to join, join to be a medicine man or a clown. And we have those.

So the head of the medicine men and the head of the clowns get together to choose the Governor. One year it is the medicine man. We still have our two sides, Summer side and the Winter side. So one year the Governor is from the Winter side, and this year he's from the Summer side. And next year we will have a Governor from the Winter side. And the same way with ones who are his Lieutenants. If the Governor is from the Summer side, his Lieutenant will be from the Winter side. And then the Second Lieutenant will be from the Summer side, and it is like that down the line—Summer, Winter, Summer, Winter. And the same way with the Scouts. They are called War Chiefs now. I don't know who changed the name, but they are called War Chiefs, and they are chosen, four of them together—or six. Anyway, we have six, I think, so three are from the Summer side and three are from the Winter side.

And having them like that we have the two groups together. This group knows what is happening over there [on the Winter side], and that group knows what is happening here [on the Summer side], so it is a group together, that works together, and it is nice. Some of the other villages have split up. I guess they do not see eye to eye, and they do not bother to get together to solve things. It is kind of sad to have the people in the village separated. When this group and this group get together and talk things over and make everything right, it is good.

"San Juan Pueblo: Winter and Summer Chiefs." Tape 5, told at the San Juan Pueblo Church for visiting students from Los Alamos High School, March 1998. Recorded by M. Ellien Carroll. Transcribed and edited by Tilar Mazzeo; edited by Sue-Ellen Jacobs, Henrietta M. Smith, and M. Ellien Carroll.

Pueblo Wedding Shower

My grandmother was always out doing something for a friend who needed help. And many a time, I asked her if I can come and help too. But she would say no, because as a child I would only get in the way, and she would not get much done.

So, this certain day, she was invited to a wedding. It was not a wedding exactly, but it was something like your wedding shower. It was something like that. Only, this is only for the relatives of the boy. There is a lot more before that. Let me tell you just a little bit.

When a boy wants to get married, it is not begging like you see nowadays. He has a roving eye and looks at all the girls. And pretty soon, maybe he will find somebody whom he likes. And he does not tell the girl. A girl knows nothing about it. He has that feeling in his heart that he likes her. So he goes and tells his parents. And his parents gather the relatives. And they talk about the girl to see whether she will make him a good wife. And I suppose the boy is sitting there with his fingers crossed. But sometimes it does not happen. Sometimes they tell him to look out and that he should go find another girl. And then maybe he finds somebody, and he goes through the same thing. But when his parents all agree on a certain girl that he likes, then the father and some of the elders on his side will go and ask for the young girl.

But that's not all of it. Now it's the girl's parents and her relatives that sit down and talk about the boy to see if he's going to make a good husband. Well, he's now sitting on pins and needles. Anything that happens that is important always takes four days. You don't rush into things. So, he waits. One day is gone. Nobody came to tell him anything. Second day. Two more days to go. He's still waiting. And then three days, gone. One more day. He sits and waits. And nobody came over to tell him anything. So that means everything is okay.

So he starts getting ready. His folks, his relatives, all help him and tell him what he has to do. It's not a wedding where you can go to a

"Pueblo Wedding Shower." Tape 13, told at the Rocky Mountain Storytelling Festival, August 7, 1998, Palmer Lake, Colo. Recorded by M. Ellien Carroll. Transcribed and edited by Tilar Mazzeo; edited by Sue-Ellen Jacobs, Henrietta M. Smith, and M. Ellien Carroll.

store and buy your gifts, buy your material to make a wedding dress. It's all up to the young man. Now, if he's a good hunter he goes up to the mountain to get a deer or an elk, and he will make the moccasins.

The moccasins are supposed to last a lifetime. Now, this one—the bottom part that I am wearing is not Indian made. They were bought in a store. My moccasins that go with this núnú?aa [Native dress] are out in Nevada somewhere. I loaned them to a niece when she was in the choir, and they had to sing their song in their Native costume. So I sent her a bunch of clothes, including the shoes. I just should have bought her store-bought moccasins. I thought they were going to come back, so I loaned them to her. And they have a little point at the end, right at the toe, like a little elf's shoes. Those are the dress-up shoes. The everyday shoes just pull on like a boot and tie at the knee. Those are the everyday shoes.

So, a woman has two pairs of shoes, and they are supposed to last her a lifetime. The way my grandmother walked around and did things, her moccasins would always wear out on the bottom. The sole would always wear out. So that kept my grandfather busy. He would take off the sole and a tiny bit of sewing that has been on it. He would cut that off, and then put on another sole. That is why they last a life-time—the boot part, the leg part lasts a lifetime, not the sole.

Sometimes, my grandfather would get angry at my grandmother because she is going here, she is going there. I think she could out-walk anybody even in this time. Because she was tiny, she was active. Always on the go. I do not know how old she was when she passed away, but she was still pretty well in shape so that she could go anywhere. She did not have a car, and she did not ride a horse, so she had to depend on her feet. And she was always going to help people or help someone far away. So my grandfather had to make the shoes, the moccasins and the shoes.

When the moccasins are done, then the man goes after wood for his own family and the little family that is going to be his soon enough. He brings wood, a load of wood for them, so that his wife-to-be will be warm, and she will have wood to burn, to cook her meals. And that is a lot of work. That is a lot of work.

So the day comes when he will have to come and invite all his people, all his relatives, to go and see the new bride-to-be, the new addition to their family. And my grandmother was invited to one of those. Well, she went to many of them, but never took me.

I always wanted to go. Because I was a nosy little girl, I always wanted to know what's going on wherever she went. She would get ready, taking her time and talking about it. So I always wanted to go. She was invited, and I asked her, "Can I go with you, grandmother?" And she thought about it. I was just a little girl, always playing in the dirt. And she told me, "Well, I will call you and you come and wash your face. And I will comb you hair." So that meant she was going to take me, she was going to take me. So she said, "Now go play outside, and do not bother anyone. I will do what I have to do." I kept coming in to check on her. I didn't want to be left behind, so I came back.

We didn't have dishes from the store to eat out of. Our dishes were all handmade, from clay. And they are not the fancy kind that you see when tourists go to the pueblos to buy. There is a lot of work put in that pottery now. A lot of work. But the pottery my grandmother made was for practical use. She had thick pots that she used for making her dough and thick pots to store her seeds for my grandfather, and they are placed right next to the wall. They are buried.

And the adobe floor—we did not have a wood floor, we had a dirt floor. And the dirt floor had to be patched every so often. It has to be patched with wet mud and then smoothed over. My hand would not be good for that. This little finger is always getting in the way. The left hand would be better. But she would do it with her hands to smooth the dirt, because she did not have a trowel. She did not have one of those to smooth the dirt, so she used her hands. And after it dries, while it is still damp, then she has a rock, a black rock. She would go over all the cracks, and that sort of pats down the dirt, so it is a nice hard floor for moccasin feet, yes, but not for shoes like that, shoes that had heels. My grandmother used to get after my little brother and I that we were like horses, running through adobe buildings.

So she called me in, and I was telling you about the dishes. My auntie, on my mother's side, her older sister, was a midwife. And she went to help the Spanish people have their babies. Hardly anybody went to hospitals. Especially my people. My people were afraid to go to a doctor. They thought when you go to a doctor, the doctor is going to get his knife and slice you open to see what is wrong with you in there. They were afraid to go to the doctor. Their herbs did the job. Sometimes just a massage.

And so when she would help, when my auntie went to help Spanish women have their babies, they would give her store-bought vegetable dishes. Those dishes had beautiful flowers on the inside. Some had gold trim. And sometimes my grandmother used to do extra things for my aunt, because she could not do a lot of the work that women do. She was sort of, I do not say crippled—she walked with a sort of a swaying motion. Then she would give my grandmother one of her bowls.

Grandmother had them up high where I would not bother them, because they are pretty. And when she was getting ready to go out, she would get one down and look at it. One had a big red rose in the middle. And then the other one had violets on it. I guess they were violets—they were something pretty. And then there is another one that had a gold trim. And then she would dust it with her sheet—or if she had an apron she would dust it with her apron and put it back up there. And she would get another one down.

I was standing there looking at all of them. I thought she was going to let me take one of those as a present. So, after a while, she decided which one she wanted to take. And there was a paper sack, and she just wrapped it up in there and set it down on the table. She said, "My that's pretty. Now I'll have to go find you one too."

And I am standing there looking at the dishes she had up there— pretty dishes. I thought she was going to let me have one. But she went in the other room. I thought she had more in there. I thought she had more. She came out dusting back the thing she was bringing out with her apron again. And she came to me, she said, "You can take this one." A canning jar. It was a poor canning jar. And I guess I looked disappointed, because I wanted one of those pretty dishes. And she said to me, "This is pretty, because you can see through it." She put it close to my eyes. Sure enough, you can see through it. And it didn't matter then, because I was going to get to go. It did not matter whether I had the pretty dishes or a canning jar for a present.

Many a time I wondered what other people took, because there was no stores. Some people were good hunters and their family would take buckskin for a present for the young bride. That I know. But I do not know the others.

So, when it was time to go, she called me. And she combed my hair and washed my face. She combed my hair, and I don't know if she put on a clean dress. But anyway, I was all excited, and we went. And we went.

The room was a long room, and the bride was standing way at the other end. She had on a turquoise dress, all down to her ankles, and beautiful black hair that hung down. And I looked at her. She reminded me of the fairy princess that I read about in the books. And I could not keep my eyes off her.

It is just the women who go, and there was a whole line. And each woman that went gives her a present and gives her a hug to welcome her to our side of the family. So the line was going slow, and I keep watching her. I look at her on both sides, and then I forget to move, so my grandmother would push me. And that is how I finally got to where the bride was standing. And she was tall. She towered over me. But I was a little girl, I don't know how small I was. And so I looked up at her. She smiled at me. And I had chills all down my back, all down my back, looking at the fairy princess. I didn't know what to do. I stood there, with my mouth wide open, and holding my canning jar in a paper sack.

I stood there and looked at her. And after a while I had that sack, and my grandmother said, "Give her the present." So I handed it to her, and she got it, but I was still frozen. I was still frozen, and I didn't know what to do. I gave her the present, and then I took off. And then Grandmother reached out and got me by the collar. Took me back and stood me in front of the young girl again, and she said, "Give her a hug." So I gave her a hug. And then I don't know what happened, but that was my experience of a shower.

Everyday Life at San Juan Pueblo

My grandfather, my grandfather was not as active as my grandmother. He was a tall man, at least I thought he was. And he was an important man in the village. In our village, we are divided into two groups: the Summer Clan and the Winter Clan. We have a Winter Chief and a Summer Chief. The Summer Chief is in charge of what goes on in the village in the summertime. And the Winter Chief is the advisor during the time the Summer Chief is chief. And then, in the fall, when everything is turned over to the Winter Chief, then the Summer Chief becomes the advisor. So that is how my people ruled.

And we have other workers in the village. We have Scouts. The Scouts were needed when the people first moved into the pueblo and sometimes several tribes would come and steal the crops from my people. Or sometimes there is a woman out where she is not supposed to be, out in a garden gathering whatever she needs to cook, and she does not know that renegades were close by. She would get taken away, or her children. So for that reason we had Scouts. There are two Scouts in the different directions. When there is something suspicious that they see, they would send one home, and the pueblo would hide the women. They have a certain building where they would hide the women and the children. And they had another place where they hid their crops after harvest. But that is the way it was.

And remember Coyote? Poor Coyote gets shot down for a lot of things in stories. But in my Indian way, anytime anybody shoots you down and calls you a name and tells you that you are no good, that person who is saying the mean things to you is giving you her good luck or his good luck. So that is the way my grandmother explained it. You do not feel bad if children mistreat you. Just say, "Thank you" and get away. So that was nice. That was nice.

And that was the way Coyote was, Coyote at one time was a little dog of the prairie. The little watchdog of the prairie. Whenever he

"Everyday Life at San Juan Pueblo." Tape 13, told at the Rocky Mountain Storytelling Festival, August 7, 1998, Palmer Lake, Colo. Recorded by M. Ellien Carroll. Transcribed and edited by Tilar Mazzeo; edited by Sue-Ellen Jacobs, Henrietta M. Smith, and M. Ellien Carroll.

howled out in the hills, people used to listen. People listened. Sometimes it is just bad weather coming along, a big snowstorm or some change of weather. And the men have to go and gather wood, or, if they have enough wood, they chop wood so they have plenty to burn. This was a time when you did not have gas, you did not have any electricity. It's just what there is in nature. Even traveling.

When you travel there were no motels, no hot dog stands, and you have to carry your lunch. This is what I would tell the children when I was teaching in the bilingual classroom. I used to ask them, "What would you do if you could not find hot dogs or potato chips when you get hungry?" And they would change to something else: "Well, we will go buy us a pizza." But I guess it is hard to understand that.

It is probably hard for you to understand that we ate out of homemade dishes, and everything was homemade, even the baskets that we use for washing wheat. The men folks always raised wheat and plenty of corn. And the wheat had to be washed before it's ground into flour,

Figure 5. San Juan Pueblo women washing wheat in Rio Grande, 1905, by Edward S. Curtis. (Courtesy Museum of New Mexico, Neg. No. 31249)

and they make huge baskets depending on the size of the woman. I use one about so big [approximately 2 feet in diameter]. And they are flat, sort of flat and go down like that. You put your wheat in there and lower it into water that is not too strong. Water that will carry away the chaff. I keep thinking of the word in my language, and I cannot think of it in your language. And sometimes we use little branches, sunflower branches and things like that are in there, and they get washed away. And that is how we wash our wheat. And the basket is also used as a strainer.

Growing up in a village like that, with so many people helping to raise children was good, was nice, very nice. You learned to know your elders. And we were taught respect, a lot of respect for the elders. And I think that is good.

Pueblo Life

I want to tell you about my dress, the dress I am wearing. The belt I am wearing has designs on the braids, because in my area water is very precious. So, because water is so precious, we have a lot of the designs that have to do with rain and the clouds. These designs here are the rainfalls. The fringes represent the rain. The moccasins. . . . If I marry a man who is a good hunter, I have shoes for the rest of my life. A long time ago, when I was growing up, Indian women did not buy their shoes in the stores. Their shoes are buckskins, so you have to be careful where you wear them. When you go through the water, they will dry out and get out of shape. But that is the way it is.

Figure 6. Woman's everyday belt, San Juan Pueblo, 1997. (Sue-Ellen Jacobs)

My grandfather never had store-bought shoes, nor did my grandmother. And during the war [World War II], when they were rationing, when they would issue out food stamps, shoe stamps, stamps for coffee and stuff like that, my grandmother wore moccasins, as did my grandfather and my mother. All three of them wore moccasins. My children were smaller. You know how rough children are with shoes. They are always wearing out their shoes, but I was lucky because I would use the shoe stamps of the people who wore moccasins. We could do that.

Figure 7. Woman's shoes and wrappers, San Juan Pueblo, 1997. (Sue-Ellen Jacobs)

"Pueblo Life." Tape 14, told at the Broward County Main Library, Fort Lauderdale, Fla., May 3, 1992. Recorded by M. Ellien Carroll. Transcribed and edited by Tilar Mazzeo; edited by Sue-Ellen Jacobs, Henrietta M. Smith, and M. Ellien Carroll.

I grew up in New Mexico, close to Santa Fe. There are a whole bunch of Pueblos right in the Rio Grande valley. My hometown is San Juan Pueblo. That is a Spanish name. When the Spanish came, we all had Indian names, but because they could not pronounce our Indian names, they gave us all Spanish names. That is where the Martinez came from.

I have a Tewa name too: "Blue Water." My daughter and I met a couple from Missouri, and they asked a lot of questions. And I got a letter from the lady addressed to "Teacher Blue Water." I thought that was cute, to get a letter all the way from Missouri still recognizing me as a teacher. I did work in the bilingual classroom, teaching the children how to speak, read, and write the language.

I live in New Mexico. I don't think I will leave. My roots are too deep. I take off, but I go back. I go back. Yes, I do go from there to tell stories. Florida is the farthest I have come. I really enjoy this place. I really enjoyed my day at the beach and all the little treasures I find out there. The way they live their lives is the same as ours.[1]

~~~·

We have a lot of dances going on in the wintertime, not only dances but storytelling. I brought a tape of a Deer Dance, because we depend so much on what nature has to provide to survive. Not only for food, but for our clothing too, the buckskin. We depend on nature in the way of food, shelter, from the skins. Even the tools. The bones are used for tools. We do not waste anything on an animal. And that is the reason why we have the dances. We have Deer Dances, Pueblo Dances, people dances. I wish I could just take you and put you in my village, so you can see some of the dances that we have.

Ours is not a lost culture. The children, the young adults are taking a lot of interest. We have too many intermarriages from other tribes or non-Natives, so the English language is spoken in the home. So that is the only drawback. But many of our young folks are interested in picking up the language, so I think it might encourage the others.

---

1. Blue Water was talking about our visit to the Seminole village. "They tell stories. We tell stories. We all have legends of what has happened before. They have their own art work. Their art work is not like ours. They're teaching their traditions."—M. Ellien Carroll.

Pollen Gathering

Pollen is something that is used in ceremonies. My grandfather was a Winter Chief, and he needed a lot of it, so my grandmother went out to pick pollen. I went with her, because I always wanted to do what she did. She would make a pottery piece that is shaped almost like a plate, and that is what she would carry. It is all polished on the inside. She would get the corn tassels at a certain time. You cannot do it at noontime, it would have to be in the morning sometime. And so she would shake them, and the pollen would fall into her pottery. Then she would keep the pollen or some of the little sacks that had the pollen in them.

The bugs that are inside the little sacks would fall into the pottery too. And, after a while, when there are too many of those bugs, she would break off a little piece of a corn tassel, sweep them out from her pottery, and then start all over again, until she has enough to fill a little bottle. So, I helped her with that.

But I don't remember exactly what time or when she did it. I did it one time, after she was gone, just to see if I could get some. It didn't work, because I was out there either too late or too early. I think it was too late. But she knew when to get the pollen.

"Pollen Gathering." Tape 5, told at the San Juan Pueblo Church for Visiting Students from Los Alamos High School, March 1998. Recorded by M. Ellien Carroll. Transcribed and edited by Tilar Mazzeo; edited by Sue-Ellen Jacobs, Henrietta M. Smith, and M. Ellien Carroll.

Working with the Old Man at the River

There was an old man, he was very old. He did not go to the gardens to work. He liked to be out in the open, not to stay at home. So he would ask the people who had little animals that had to be fed to take them to the river where there are a lot of weeds that they can eat. Mostly it is sheep and goats that he would take. We would see him going by every day with his little flour sack of lunch over his shoulder. He would be walking with a cane on one side, and the sheep would be eating on the roadside as he took them to the river. One day I thought that would be a nice way to spend the day, with the old man. We could help him, and maybe he would tell us some stories.

So I asked my grandmother if it was all right if we followed the old man to the river with the herd that he was caring for. There were not very many—maybe there were about ten of the animals that he took to the river. So she said, "It's okay, just mind what he tells you to do: do not be disobedient, and do whatever he tells you." So we went along with him.

We asked my grandmother to fix us lunch and put it in a flour sack, so we could carry it like he carried his. I guess it was just mostly bread—maybe an apple now and then, and we would put it on our shoulder and take it.

When we got to the river, there was a big log. He would sit on that log, sit with his eyes closed and sing a song, just sit there and sing. And we would sit with him on the log, and just listen to him sing. After a while, maybe we want to swim in the river. The river is deep, but there is a side where the water just comes above your ankles, so we asked him, "Is it okay if we get in the water?" And he said, "Go cool off children, go cool off. But just stay where you see the sand. Do not go any further, just stay where you can see the sand." So we undressed, and we just played around in that little spot, my little brother and I. Then we

"Working with the Old Man at the River." Tape 4, told at STORYFIESTA™, Albuquerque, 1997. Recorded by M. Ellien Carroll. Transcribed and edited by Tilar Mazzeo; edited by Sue-Ellen Jacobs, Henrietta M. Smith, and M. Ellien Carroll.

lay down in the sand so that the water just covered our bellies, that's all it covered. We would splash around and play in it.

Then, when it was time to eat, he would call us. We would get out of the river and then put on our clothes again, and then we would sit on the log. We would wait for him to open his sack, to see what he brought for lunch. After we had seen what he had, then we opened ours up. Then we would tell him, "We brought lunch too." So we would share. We would share his lunch and ours, and sit there and eat and talk. Then we would tell him, "When you are tired, we will watch the animals so that you can take a nap." He liked that. He liked that.

When he's going to take a nap, he says, "Children, you keep an eye on the animals, I am going to rest a while." That log that he was sitting on was a big one, so he just put his blanket there and lay down, and he would take a nap. We would play quietly. We would sit in the sand and just play guessing games so we won't make noise and wake him up. And we watch the animals. They never go anywhere, because they have a lot to eat. We just sit and look at them to see that they are all there until he gets up.

When it's almost sunset, he would tell us, "Round up the animals so we can get started home. We have got to get there before supper time." So my brother goes on one side, I go on the other side, and we round them up in no time and get them on the road. They are headed home again, and we go. We help carry whatever lunch the old man had left over, so he will not have to carry it. We just walk on home then.

That is the day's work. It is his job, what he likes to do—to spend the time this way, so he does not have to be just sitting down, doing nothing in his house. He tries. He is still trying to make himself useful. There was another old man, much older than this one, and he wore pants, white pants. They were white pants, only they were made with flour sacks. People bought flour sacks that had a pansy flower on it, that was Pansy Flour; and then there was another kind of flour that was called Blue Jay and one called Bobolink, and the pictures always stayed on it. They never washed out. So when they made pants for the old men, the bobolink or the pansy would be on the end, or the bird, but that is how they were. They wore them for pants, and this old man always wore flour-sack pants.

He liked to work in the garden. He had two canes to walk with. That way, he can hold on to both of them as he walked. He had to walk quite a ways to get to his fields. He does not hoe his garden. He will sit on the ground and pull the weeds around the plants that they had planted. He would sit there and pull the weeds and get them all cleared, and he doesn't do in between—just where the plants are. That was *his* job, and he enjoyed doing that. Sometimes, when the wind is a little bit too strong, even if he is walking with a cane, holding on to the cane, the wind would blow him so that he would have to run. And he still got along. I don't know if I can do that work in the garden—especially walk as far as he had to walk. People did that.

Sheepherding

My grandfather is the one I listened to when I was growing up, and I always went to him for stories. And he never, ever, got tired of telling me stories. My grandfather lived in San Juan Pueblo all his life, except those days, when he was younger, and he went sheepherding. And that was nice. He was herding sheep in the wintertime, and it was a different way of living. It snows a lot in the wintertime, and sheep have to be taken care of even in the wintertime. And I think there were about three of them who took care of somebody's sheep. He did not say whose sheep they were.

In the wintertime, when it snowed, they would get cold, and this was a time when there were no sleeping bags. No sleeping bags, and no tents to keep the snow away. But when you find yourself in the need, you always figure out a way. He made his own sleeping bag. I guess all the guys who herded sheep made their own sleeping bags. Every time they butcher, they would tan the hide until it is soft. And the side that had the wool would go to the inside of the sleeping bag. They sewed together so many hides, depending on how big the person was. I am glad that I was not a sheepherder then. I do not know how many I would have to sew! My grandfather had his sleeping bag so the inside, the wool part, was on his body to keep him warm. The outside was waterproof. Let it snow, let it snow. He never got wet.

Another thing—before they went off to work, they always dug a little trench, just as wide as a person, so they could fit in there. And then they would build fires inside that trench. That is their bed. Their sleeping bag is rolled up so it does not get wet on the inside. They build a fire there, and put logs there, so it burns, burns, burns. By the time they are ready to go to bed, that place is hot and warm, with coals, hot coals. And then they pile green branches on top, and then they put something else on top to smother that. I think the dirt goes first on

"Sheepherding." Tape 10, told to Native American Librarians at the New Mexico Library Association Roundtable, Santa Fe, May 19, 1998. Recorded by M. Ellien Carroll. Transcribed and edited by Tilar Mazzeo; edited by Sue-Ellen Jacobs, Henrietta M. Smith, and M. Ellien Carroll.

the hot ashes, and then the green grass, and then their sleeping bag goes on there to cover up. Well, that is how they sleep in there, nice and warm. All the hot coals keep them warm all night long. How brave they are to be able to take care of themselves like that!

My grandfather had a little puppy dog who helped him with his sheep. He would follow my grandfather around wherever he went, to round up the sheep when they were going to put them back into the corral. The men who worked with my grandfather would hide the sheep sometimes. They take them up and hide the sheep somewhere. And then my grandfather would say, "Go find my sheep." He talked to the puppy dog in Indian, because he does not speak English or Spanish. But the horsemen know that even little doggies are bilingual. They can understand the bark of another dog, or they can understand Tewa too. They talk to them in Navajo all the time. So my grandfather would tell his little dog: "Dín nuwá naví k'úwá" [go find my sheep]. And the dog would wag his tail and go look for the sheep where they had wandered off. And I do not know what the puppy's name was. I am sure he had a name for his dog.

Corn Grinding Stories

1. GRINDING THE CORN

My grandmother was my teacher at the time I was a little girl. We used a lot of corn and cornmeal. It is the Indian corn that you use to cook in the oven. A whole wagonload would go in the oven, for chicos. Chicos are just fresh corn, roasted on hot ashes. But when you take the kernels off the corn cob and boil it, it has a different taste. It is not like fresh corn in the soup; it has a different taste. You can have corn-on-the-cob any time you want in the wintertime, because, when it comes out from the oven, you husk it. But you leave some of the husk on there, and, when it is all done, then you braid it up, you braid it up into long braids. Then you hang them over a pole to dry. So, whenever you want corn, then you can break off an ear and reboil it, and that is your corn-on-the-cob during the wintertimes, when there is no fresh corn.

That is the way we stored our food. Because there was no electricity, no gas, no running water. We got our drinking water from wells in the village. We were talking about the corn, and we used the corn for different things. We had corn-on-the-cob, and then you have parched corn. Parched corn is just toasted in the outside oven, where you build a fire, then take all the ashes out, and on that hot floor you throw a whole gunnysack of blue corn. My grandmother and my grandfather would stir it back and forth, back and forth, until they are ready to come out. Then that is ground, for atole or corn bread. Chicos are used for corn-on-the-cob and soup. Then there is another one that is boiled with white stuff that you dig out from the ground [lime], and you put it in with the corn, and it takes off the skin. After a while, when the skin is off the kernels of corn and that is ready, you can use that in soup, posole soup. They open up like popcorn when they boil. You can use the very fine grind for tamales, and that is good.

"Grinding the Corn" (story version 1). Tape 4, told at STORYFIESTA™, Albuquerque, 1997. Recorded by M. Ellien Carroll. Transcribed and edited by Tilar Mazzeo; edited by Sue-Ellen Jacobs, Henrietta M. Smith, and M. Ellien Carroll. We have included more than one version of corn grinding stories to show how I vary the details of events according to my audience and how I am inspired to tell the story at the time.

Figure 8. Braiding corn, San Juan Pueblo, 1935, by T. Harmon Parkhurst. (Courtesy Museum of New Mexico, Neg. No. 3975)

When a lady is out of cornmeal, she would tell maybe her neighbor—just somebody, anybody—to let them know that she is out of cornmeal. So, she has her corn all ready for grinding, and the people in the village pick a day to grind her corn. That means that the men have to come and sing. They come with their drums; it is a social gathering, and the women go and grind.

Many a time, my grandmother would be going to grind, and I would say, "Can I go with you to help grind the corn?" And she would tell me, "You have to get first stronger arms." Then I would show her: "I have muscles." But that was not enough. Then, one day, there was a lady right next door to my grandmother who needed corn.

Figure 9. Dwarf blue corn, 1998. (Sue-Ellen Jacobs)

The lady next door needed corn ground, so my grandmother told me, "Tonight you can go to help grind." And I was so tickled. I was

Figure 10. Grinding corn, San Juan Pueblo, 1935, by T. Harmon Parkhurst. (Courtesy Museum of New Mexico, Neg. No. 3971)

going to get to grind corn. I didn't know how to grind. I see her, I see her grinding tamale corn, dried corn for tamales. She would sit there and grind, and it is a nice job, with dough coming up on that side. See, you have your corn there, and the dough is coming up on the other side, and that is what we use for tamales. Well, she let me go with her.

She followed a lady who got tired grinding. I think she was there already before, but she was tired, so she got up. And my grandmother sat down to grind there. I was still waiting, standing by the door, waiting, and she probably told the lady sitting next to her to let me sit there so I could grind. I sat down by her. I was all tickled, and I got that top rock that goes down to grind the corn—the big rock that is under there, and that is where you grind the corn.

So the men sang, and when the men sing the women start grinding, and they have to keep in time with the song. It is a dance they are doing, and the men are singing for them. So I sat down, and I didn't put any corn there. I did not have sense yet, so when I sat down, I started rubbing the two rocks together. I didn't know how I was going to get cornmeal, but I wanted to show my grandmother that I could work fast, so she wouldn't say no to me the next time I wanted to go with her somewhere. But I wasn't grinding, just rubbing the two rocks together. So she elbowed me, and she said, "Put some corn on your rock to grind." She did it herself. She got some corn and put some on my stone to grind. So when they started singing, she went at hers. But I didn't watch; I should have watched. So I went at it again. I wasn't keeping time with the drummer, and she elbowed me again and said, "Listen to the drumbeat, and you keep time with the drum." Then she said, "Move your head with the drum." So I said, "Okay, okay," so she put the corn there.

Two orders she told me to do: to keep time with the drum and to move my head too. Well, one ear heard one thing, the other ear heard another thing. I said "Okay." I was going to do it right. They started singing, and I did keep time with the drum, but my head was not moving. I was looking around. She elbowed me and said, "Move your head too," so I did, I did. I would go down with drum, and I would think of my head, then I would grind some more. But the corn was not getting ground. It was just the two rocks that were getting rubbed together. So, after a while, she elbowed me and said, "You had better go, you are wasting time." So I got fired from my first job.

If my grandmother had explained to me how to grind, how she grinded. Maybe she thought I knew, thought I watched her grind the tamale dough. And I did watch her, but not enough. I didn't really watch, maybe I watched with one eye shut.

2. GRINDING THE CORN

Cornmeal was very important in the diet of my Indian people, and, in my village, when a lady would run out of cornmeal, she would tell her neighbor or somebody, and then they would pass the word around. Then the village would set a certain night to grind. Grinding corn was a way of socializing for people in the village. It was a good way to get together and to help the person who needs her corn ground. The men

"Grinding the Corn" (story version 2). Tape 5, told at the San Juan Pueblo Church for visiting students from Los Alamos High School, March 1998. Recorded by M. Ellien Carroll. Transcribed and edited by Tila Mazzeo; edited by Sue-Ellen Jacobs, Henrietta M. Smith, and M. Ellien Carroll.

would come with their drums. They sing a song,[1] and the women would keep time with the drumbeat. It is just like singing the harvest song, because the harvest song is not "Grinding, grinding, grinding," all the time. It is: "Grind, grind, stop. Grind, grind, stop." You have to keep time with the drumbeat.

And as a little girl I asked my grandmother if I could go help with the grinding whenever she went to grind corn. She always said, "No." She said, "You are not big enough. Your arms are not strong enough." Like any child would, I showed her my muscles. I would tell her, "Yes, I am strong." I showed her my muscles. But she said, "Not yet."

But I think she was waiting for a time when the grinding would take place closer to her house. Then, if I fell asleep, I wouldn't have to walk so far. If I went over on the other side of the village to grind, I would have to come all the way back to the middle houses to go to bed. We lived there, and one day there was a lady right next door who wanted corn. And so, when she was going to grind, my grandmother said, "Tonight you can go help." I was so tickled, because for once I was going to do a grown-up job. I thought I was big enough to do a job. But, like I said, I was a tag-along too, and I was just a little girl— maybe six or seven. I was small.

They were going to grind there, and so she said, "When I am ready to go, I will call you, and you can come in and wash your face. And I will comb your hair." I had long hair, so she braided it. And I had bangs. She had my bangs cut. So, when she was ready to go, she called me in. I was staying out with the kids. So I went and washed my face, and she combéd my hair.

---

1. The English translation of the song is:

> "The little corn are being
> ground, ground;
> They are like little popcorn,
> small like popcorn;
> As you grind they pop,
> And they go pop
> this way and that way."

My Auntie would also sing this song as a lullaby to me and the other children. We would climb up on her lap one at a time and she would sing. [From the end of tape 2, March 2000 tapes; transcribed by Sue-Ellen Jacobs, January 7, 2003.]

But she did not tell me what I was supposed to do. I knew the ladies sat at the grinding stones and moved the rocks up, back and forth. But she did not tell me I was supposed to put corn on the rocks to grind, and she did not tell me how to hold the top rock. I was just anxious to go, and we went. There was a row of ladies on one side of the wall there—about seven. The women were grinding, and the men with their drums were sitting at one end, singing their songs and beating their drums. So you are supposed to keep time with the drumbeat, and she did not tell me that either. I knew they sang, but I did not know we were supposed to keep up with the drumbeat.

So, when one of the ladies was grinding, she got tired, and she stood up, and my grandmother sat in her place. There was another lady sitting next to her, and I think my grandmother whispered to her to let me have her place. So, after a little while, my grandmother called me, and I went, and I sat down. And I thought I was smart. I thought I was smart. I thought I knew it all. But I didn't. So I sat down and got the rock that went on top and started grinding. I was just moving it over the other rock that was there. I started moving it, and she said, "Not yet, you wait till they start singing." So when they started beating the drums, I got hold of my rock and waited for the song. When they started singing, I moved it again. And she looked. I didn't have any corn on my rock. I wasn't doing the job I was supposed to do, to help grind. I was just moving the rock over the bigger rock. And so she elbowed me, and she said, "Put some corn on your rock so you can grind something." Well, the corn assistant got some, and put it on my rock.

But she didn't show me how I was supposed to handle this top one. So when they were singing I went at it again, and that just pushed the corn off my big rock. But I was still working the top rock. She saw again that I was not working, and so she put some more corn on my rock. And then she told me, "Hold your rock up so that it picks up some of the kernels, and then press down." Well, I did that. But I was working without listening to the drumbeat. I was really working. I wanted to show her that I could do the job, so I was really just going at my own speed, not with the drumbeat. And she elbowed me again, and she said, "Keep up with the drumbeat and move your head too. You are supposed to move your head when you grind."

That was a little too much to remember. Put corn on the rock, and lift it up to catch the corn to grind. Now she says I am supposed to keep time with the drumbeat and move my head too. I had too much to remember at one time! So I would grind, and then I would remember that I am supposed to move my head—sometimes a little too late, so my rock would go down. Then I would remember my head, and I would move it a little too late for the drumbeat. Then I am working again, and I would remember that I am supposed to move my head, and I would move it again. I guess I was just making a monkey of myself there. And then my grandmother looked, and I wasn't doing a good job. So she elbowed me and said, "You'd better let somebody else sit there." So I got fired from my first job.

But it was nice. That was a nice social gathering for the people in the village. Many of the people in the village here had the grinding stones, and there were rows of houses. There were some way over to that end that had a row of grinding stones, and they had many on this side too. So, if they wanted to grind, they just asked the lady who owned the place where they had the grinding stones if they can use it. And then there is a big pot of whatever it is they cook outside. Whenever the men get tired of singing, they have other men to change around with. The bunch that is singing gets tired, and another group would come and sing. So they change often. It is the same with the ladies who were grinding. And then, after some time, they have a break, and they all have whatever is cooking out front. I never stayed awake long enough to share what they had cooking. But the people who were waiting outside would keep up with the fire, and they had a big pot, a cooking pot made out of pottery.

My people did not have store-bought stuff to cook in or to eat out of. We had pottery made for cooking and pottery to eat out of, pottery where my grandmother would mix her dough. And there was pottery made for storage. So everything was handmade. And beans, when cooking in the pot, might taste of the clay that is used for making the cooking pot. It always comes out so red, a different color than things you cook in another kind of a pot.

Another thing that I remember too, as I grew up, was when they are husking corn. That was a good time, too, for people to get together.

People helped one another. Everything was community work. Maybe this man had a lot of corn to husk and somebody else over there did not plant any, because he does not like to work in the fields, and he did something else. He and his family will come and help over here. And they were given corn. They took time husking their corn, because the women always make sure that they took the best husks for tamale husks. Indian corn is always about so long [10–14 inches], and the husks are about that [4–6 inches] wide, so they make good tamale husks. And if you just peel them in a hurry, you split the cornhusks. The cornhusks split. So you had to pull them off one at a time, and that is time-consuming. But that is the way they did it. And they would save tamale husks for themselves. And sometimes they would come across a pretty ear of corn that they like and want to keep. So they just fold the husk back and put it on their side, because they are taking that home. The rest of the corn that is getting husked gets thrown in a different pile, but what you want to take home you put on the side, along with the tamale husks.

The cornhusk was also used—that is, the thin, the real thin husk—was used for smoking tobacco. My grandfather raised tobacco. Not a lot, maybe about five plants, and my grandmother did the drying. I used to help her when she was picking her leaves. I do not know which ones she picked. She does not pick all of them from one spot, just certain ones, and I go by her side. She would put them in my hand, and I would carry them. Sometimes, we would find a big tomato worm. I do not like the looks of a tomato worm. Sometimes she would see a tobacco leaf with a tomato worm on it, and she would put it in my hand. I would get scared. I do not like it, so I would drop her leaves, and then I would get scolded. I would have to pick the leaves up one by one, to make them just the way she had them, because, when she lay them out to dry, they had to be just so. You do not just throw them together. That was one thing that we did.

Figure 11. Husking and braiding corn, San Juan Pueblo, 1935, by T. Harmon Parkhurst. (Courtesy Museum of New Mexico, Neg. No. 3984)

Figure 12. Juanita Trujillo sorting "Indian corn" at San Juan Pueblo, 1935, by T. Harmon Parkhurst. (Courtesy Museum of New Mexico, Neg. No. 4054)

3. GRINDING THE CORN

When we are at the village, my grandmother is the one who taught me lots of things. Once in a while, she would make buwá bread, also known as piki bread. Buwá bread is made with cornmeal. My grandmother always used a big cornmeal stone. In those days, we did not have a flour mill to take the corn and grind it up. The women have to grind it up by hand. But it is not such a hard job, because it is a social gathering. When they gather there, with all the women who want to grind corn, they would grind for whoever wants flour.

And the buwá bread is just atole and mustard. It is like a corn bread. You fix it like you would posole and then grind it up. The atole flour is roasted in the oven like you roast khúu̜ [corn] or piñon seeds. A whole sack is put in the outside oven and roasted and then ground up. That is what you use for buwá bread. You have the dough on your hands, and you put it on your hands and run it over the hot stone that is supposed to be the grill for making the bread. And you have to know how to go over it fast, so you do not burn your hands. That is what my grandmother taught.

She also taught me how to grind. For grinding, I was not allowed to go with her until I was a little older. She would say, "Wait until you grow bigger and you are stronger." Well, I thought I was strong enough. I would show her my arms and say, "I am strong, I am strong." But the reason why she never took me to grind was because she had to grind on the other side of the arroyo or somewhere else.

One day, there was a lady who wanted to grind right next door to her. So she said, "You can help me grind. You can go help me grind tonight. Go wash your face, and I will comb your hair." So I went and washed my face and combed my hair, and we went next door.

The men always sang songs and beat on the drums for the time. The women sat in a row, and they grind to the sound of the drumbeat. I did not know that, and she did not tell me. She thought I knew, because I always wanted to go. And so she was sitting there grinding and let me

"Grinding the Corn" (story version 3). Tape 9, told at the Van Buren Middle School, Albuquerque, 1997. Recorded by M. Ellien Carroll. Transcribed and edited by Tilar Mazzeo; edited by Sue-Ellen Jacobs, Henrietta M. Smith, and M. Ellien Carroll.

Figure 13. Three San Juan Puebio women grinding meal, one waiting to take her turn. (Courtesy Museum of New Mexico, Neg. No. 47250)

sit by her. There was a lady sitting by her, but I guess she wanted me to sit there, so she asked her to let me sit there and grind right by her.

Because I wanted to show her that I know how to grind, I went to work. But all I did was rub the two rocks together. I was not grinding anything, but I thought I was. I went at it fast, and I was so proud that I could do that. She elbowed me, and she said, "Put the corn on your rock, and then grind." I didn't have any corn. And so she grabbed ahold of some corn and put it on my rock. But she didn't tell me how to use the top stone.

When they started singing, she said to me: "You keep time with the song. You keep time with the drumbeat." So, when they sang, I went at it again, at the drumbeat. I thought I was doing it okay. But what I was doing was pushing the corn away from the rock. I wasn't holding my rock the way that I should. You are supposed to hold it up and catch the corn and then go down and crack. And I didn't know that. So then, she elbowed me again: "That song that they are singing, you are supposed to be grinding then. You are supposed to keep time with the drumbeat and keep moving your head with the drum."

I thought I had everything in my head. I tried so hard. While I was grinding, I kept time with my arms, trying to keep up with the drumbeat. But I forgot to move my head, or I moved it after I had moved my hands. Then I remembered to move my head. So this arm goes down and then my head. I was sitting there, just making a monkey of myself, and after a while she elbowed me and said, "You better leave that grinding stone so somebody else can grind, because you are just wasting time." So I got fired from my first job.

Cornhusking Traditions

The cornhusking is another time of social gathering. Not for the whole village, but just for the different groups that come and help out. And we had traditions. If a man peels a corn that has no kernels on it, he will find a wife sitting there helping and spank her with that corn cob and tell her, "You are a lazy cook. You did not feed your husband enough, so he did not raise a good crop." And if she gets the empty corn cob, she will do the same to him. She would spank him with that corn cob that does not have any kernels on it and tell him he is a lazy man, he was not irrigating his corn field the way he should be irrigating it, so that is why it did not have corn on that corn ear. So, it is just for fun. And sometimes, when it is a young couple, then the lady will get up and run away before he is ready to spank her with it, when she sees him hurrying up with that empty ear of corn. She knows already what is going to happen, so she takes off, and they go chasing all over the place. And then, finally, he will catch her and spank her wherever he catches her. That is part of custom.

There is another one that has to do with planting. This happens when they plant corn in the springtime. The men are going to plow up their land. They are carrying their corn seeds in a wagon. The women are waiting in the doorway with a dipper full of water! But the men know this, and so they watch. If they see a doorway open a bit when they get there, they make the horses go faster. If a man does not know this and does not make his horses run, then the lady would pull open the door and throw the dipper full of water at him, and he is all wet by the time he gets out of the village. But that is only to give him a good year, so that he has plenty of rain to moisten his seeds during the summer time. So he gets some wetness first, before he even starts. And I thought that was such fun.

One day, when my grandfather was going to plant, my little brother

---

"Cornhusking Traditions." Tape 5, told at San Juan Pueblo for visiting students. Recorded by M. Ellien Carroll. Transcribed and edited by Tilar Mazzeo; edited by Sue-Ellen Jacobs, Henrietta M. Smith, and M. Ellien Carroll.

and I wanted just to watch. We were nosy. We just wanted to see my grandfather get all that water on him. We did not have rugs, so we put a little goatskin on the bottom of the wagon. We sat on that. So we were peeking out to see the houses that had their doors maybe open, and to see if my little brother sees one. We wanted Grandfather to get wet, so we waited for them to throw the water. Anyway, this lady had a dipper of water and was waiting, and my grandfather saw her. So he made his horses run, but they were not going fast enough. So she threw that dipper of water. And the two nosy ones were in the back of the wagon, holding on to the seat. My grandfather was sitting there, and we were standing here. We were going to watch him get wet! So we stood there, and he ducked! So he didn't get the water, but we got the water. We got the water in our faces and all down our shirts. That was fun. Because Grandfather did not get wet, *we* got wet! So we had to work with him all wet. This is another thing that Indian people used to do, but they do not do that anymore. No longer is there the spanking of the women when they husk corn.

Naví Pʼôeʔą́ä
(My Life's Path)

Life with Mom and Dad in Ute Country

I was born at a time when there were no cars, just wagons. My father was working in the government boarding school in Ute country. This was in Colorado. Today you can make the trip in a car in a day; but at that time, in a wagon, I thought it was so far, so far. And that was where my father worked. As a farmer, he planted the school garden. He planted a lot of potatoes. It was just a small garden for the school to use in the kitchen—radishes, cabbages, and potatoes, things like that. He was also the dairyman. When he went in to milk the cows, I always had a little tin. He would just milk the cow right into my cup, and I would drink my milk fresh. And he was a night watchman too.

This was a time when I was not yet going to school; I was still playing stick horse with my young brother. We would ride the stick horses—not the store-bought ones, but we would get a willow branch and ride them. I think maybe I was too big a headache for my mother. She had a back door and a front door; and when her house was nice and clean, her little rugs put down, everything in order, here we came with our stick horses, my little brother following me. I didn't know that I was doing wrong; it was fun to have to go through a tunnel, riding a big willow with a bushy tail. See, the leaves are still on that willow branch, and that was supposed to be the tail. Can you imagine as we ran from the living room door, through the kitchen door, out the back way, taking the rugs along with us, so they piled up on the floor at the

"Life with Mom and Dad in Ute Country." Tape 4, told at STORYFIESTA™, Albuquerque, 1997. Recorded by M. Ellien Carroll. Transcribed and edited by Tilar Mazzeo; edited by Sue-Ellen Jacobs, Henrietta M. Smith, and M. Ellien Carroll.

back door of the house? That was our play. And maybe that is why she agreed to let me go to the boarding school.

I had two older sisters, and the oldest one was already there. Then it was time for my other sister to go. I thought it was a good advantage to be able to go to a boarding school and stay there all day long, even in the night time. So I asked my dad if I could go to school. He told me I was not ready yet, but I kept pestering, and pretty soon my mother said, "Let her go, let her go. I think she will be all right, but if she cries you bring her back home." Well, I went. It was nice.

I did a lot of tagging along behind my father then. I don't really remember the classroom, so I guess I didn't spend a lot of time in the classroom. But I might have. That is what I did—I followed him to the school garden, and I followed him to his dairy to get my share of milk. Then, when it was time to go home, I had my own little bed. That was when they felt I would cry, in the night time. When I first went, they were trying me out to see if I would cry.

At the stores, they used to sell gingersnaps in little barrel-like boxes, and my father would buy a box of gingersnaps. He had it put away. During the night time, he would stick two gingersnaps under my pillow when he came around to see that the little girls are okay. Sometimes we would kick off our covers or they fall off the bed, and my father would go around to see that the little girls were all right. I never heard him when he came, but I would always see the two gingersnaps under there, so I was anxious to go to bed. I would sleep all night long. There is nothing to cry about—not then. The next morning I peep under my pillow, and there are two gingersnaps. That is what I go for, and that starts my day. It was nice.

While I was there, I do not think I went to school long, though I do not remember. Like I say, I don't remember the classroom, but I remember a lady who was my teacher. When my father took me in and told her that I was going home with my grandparents, she wrote a note. I could not read yet then, so I don't know what she said. She gave the note to my grandfather before we left, and she said, "When you take her to San Juan and when she goes to the state school, make sure you give this note to the teacher." So we went.

When my grandfather and grandmother had come to visit my

mother, I asked if I could go home with them, because I just wanted a wagon ride, in a covered wagon. I didn't know how far it was. So my grandmother said, "Let her go. I need a little girl in the house to do errands for me or to help me out with little things." So that was all right. Since I didn't cry in the classroom, I would be all right on the trip home.

It was the nicest, nicest trip. I rode in a wagon. My grandfather would lay a bunch of hay in the bottom of the wagon box and then a homemade mattress. We never had a bought mattress, and we never had any beds. The rolled-up mattresses were made like a big sack, and on either side there was a string on the inside of the sack. You stuff a roll of wool inside, and then you tie it up, and that holds the wool together. So that is our mattress. And those mattresses could be taken apart. The outside could be washed, and you can take it apart to wash the wool on the inside too, then fluff it up and stuff it again. So they were nice. Anyway, that is what he had in the wagon box.

I don't know where they carried the food, but my grandmother always had a box of food that she would fix on the way. We would stop by on the roadside when my grandfather would get hungry. We would stop, and then Grandmother would build a fire and cook something to eat for all of us. She always made oven bread, so we could have bread on the way. But if my grandfather wanted hot tortillas, she would fix just a little dough, just enough to make two or three tortillas. She did not have a grill on the road, so she would build a fire on the ground. When there are hot coals, she would put her tortillas right on the hot coals. Those are nice. They were nice.

The trails that wagons followed were trails that cowboys and horseback riders made. See, the men always went first on horseback, and, if they wanted to go on the other side of the mountain, then they would climb up the mountain and go down the other side. They always followed a short cut. So, after a while, that horse trail is there for people to go on horseback. And then, when the wagon wants to go to the other side, it follows the horse trail. And that is how roads became—a short cut, then a wagon road over dirt. None of it was paved, none of it was gravel, and remember I said that sometimes a wagon would ride over a hill and other times it would go around it? But it was fun. It was fun.

In places where it was rough like that, sometimes I liked to explore.

I don't like to sit in a wagon box, kind of sitting sideways. I would go down from the wagon box and just hang on to the wagon box or walk in back. Whenever my grandfather stopped for the night, it was the same thing with the wagon box and the food we had that Grandmother would fix us. She would fix the food.

In those times there were no motels. You do not see any riders or any travelers on the road. A lot of the time, you are the only people riding in a wagon for as far as you can see. And, like I said, there are no motels to sleep in. There were no hot dog stands. You were there all alone. But you did not miss them. I did not know what hot dogs were, I did not know what french fries were, nor did I know what candy was. And so, when you don't know these things, you don't miss them. At dark, when we stopped for the night, my grandmother would put a mattress down for her and my grandfather. I was little, so I didn't feel anything. I could sleep on the dirt floor—as long as I had a cover, I would be okay. She always put out a blanket for me to lay on. First goes a canvas to cover the dirt, and then a mattress, and then my blanket on the side, and she would cover me up. I guess we never got caught in the rain during the night time. It was so nice to lay there and look at the stars. The stars were always bright. Once in awhile, you would see one shooting across the sky, and watching the sky you would fall asleep.

The next morning, when I would wake up, I would wake up to the smell of a fire burning. My grandparents would get up before I do— I suppose to fix breakfast. We would eat, and then we would go on our way after. I really don't know how long it took. I only know that it is a long way for a little girl to ride with these two elderly people. I cannot play with my grandmother, and I cannot play with my grandfather. See, I would like to run after them and play tag, but they were past the age of playing tag. So I found my own friends to play with, and the things I played with were grass.

There was a lot of grass that grew in bunches, and I would get the grass and braid up the grass like it was hair. I would talk to the grass like my grandmother did to me. She would tell me, "You be a nice little girl, and respect the elders. Do what you're told to do, and don't talk back." So, while I was braiding that grass, I would talk to my make-believe little sister when I was braiding her hair. When I had braided her grass hair, I found the yarn. This is how my grandmother used to tie my hair—with yarn, sometimes with a green yarn, sometimes with a red yarn. When I get through braiding the grass up, I would tie a bunch of her "hair" with a yarn, and I would say, "Now go play." Then I would find me another one. And, after I had made that one, I would say, "You do what your sister tells you. Go where your sister takes you, and don't be running away." Then I had two make-believe sisters to talk to on the wagon, and there I can play house. I had two grass children. So that was how we played going on the wagon.

Moving by Wagon from Ute Country
to Tewa Country

My grandparents both lived in San Juan Pueblo, in the village, and every year they would go to visit my folks to see how they are doing. It was during one of those visits that I wanted to take a wagon ride. At that time there were hardly any cars. I do not remember seeing very many cars. So it was during one of the times when my grandparents went to visit my folks that I wanted to go home with them in the covered wagon. I did not realize how far it was to travel in a covered wagon.

In a car, you can make it in a day to Ute country, easy. But in that covered wagon, my grandfather always makes his horses go slow, just at a walking speed, that is all. He never makes them trot, he never makes them run, so that is how slowly we travel. It is a time when there were no houses on the roadside. You are there on the road, on the little dirt road, all by yourself, as far as you can see, just you and your grandparents and the horses, on the road. Once in a while, maybe there might be someone on horseback going someplace, but that is just someone going off to somewhere else, going to follow a trail.

These wagon trails that came about were made by the horse riders. Anyone going someplace always finds the shortest way to go, and usually you can do that on horseback. So the horse trails are what the wagons follow. None of them were paved; they were just dirt roads. On windy days they were dusty, and when it rains they get muddy. But it was fun.

My grandfather had the cover on the wagon, and, if we had a nice day, he would tie a rope around the canvas covering so we can look up to the sky. But if it is raining, then that got let down, and we are inside the covered wagon, all cooped up. I did not like that; I liked to look out.

When you are going in a covered wagon, you can look out and see the little animals on the roadside: you see chipmunks, you see squir-

"Moving by Wagon from Ute Country to Tewa Country." Tape 4, told at STORYFIESTA™, Albuquerque, 1997. Recorded by M. Ellien Carroll. Transcribed and edited by Tilar Mazzeo; edited by Sue-Ellen Jacobs, Henrietta M. Smith, and M. Ellien Carroll.

rels running into the grass, you see bugs and little beetles trying to get away from the wagon wheel. And that was nice, because I was just a little girl. And remember I asked to tag along, and my mother let me go with my grandmother so I could help her with whatever chores she had for a little girl to do.

So we would go on the road. When we got hungry, my grandmother had her stash of food. Tortillas were made right on the spot. If we wanted tortillas, they were made right over the campfire, on the hot coals. But my mother would make bread for us to take along on the trip too, and that is what we had—and whatever else my grandma would carry for lunch. We had that as we went along.

My grandmother did not like to sit in the front seat where my grandfather rode, and I guess I would like sitting there. I liked the wagon box, because, when I got tired of sitting or talking to my grandmother, then I would go down the back end of the wagon, and I would hang onto the wagon box and run. Or sometimes she gets tired and starts dozing off, and she would lay down in the wagon box and go to sleep. Sometimes I would go chase after maybe a lizard in the grass or a chipmunk. I never caught them, because they are always fast.

Once in a while on the roadside, there is a beetle—those little beetles that hold their hind end up. I saw one standing, just running into the grass, and I tapped it, because I was not sure whether it was going to bite or not. I tapped it on the back, and then it put its hind end up and its head down to the bottom. It tickled me so. And it had a funny odor; it was a stink bug.

So, that stink bug just stood there, and I would ask my grandfather, "What is it doing standing on its head?" He said, "Be quiet, it is listening to what is going on down below." So I would try to listen, but I do not hear anything. So, I just look at the bug, and then I would ask my grandfather, "What is that bug hearing?" And he said, "Well, they are talking about Coyote, they are telling the men to gather all the fast-running horses and round up the coyotes." So that is what the pheḍápusabeʔ is doing, listening. A "stink bug" is not a "stink bug" in my language: it is called a pheḍápusabeʔ. It just has its hind end up and listening.

So that is what I looked for mostly on the roadways—a bug, a beetle that I can tap and maybe it will put its hind end up. A lot of times they do not, a lot of times maybe it is a cricket. I will want to tap it, and then it jumps out of the way. But it was nice. Those were my playthings. I did not have any playthings to play with; I did not have a doll, and so I had to find my own toys.

When night time comes, my grandmother would build a fire right under a tree on the road. I forgot to tell you, the roads were just in the open country. There were no fences. Everything was open country. You can park any place you want on the road side. My grandfather would turn his horses loose. He always picks a place where there is a stream of running water so his horses can drink and have plenty of grass to eat. So he turned them loose.

My grandmother would build a fire and cook supper. Whatever she fixed, we would eat. I do not remember what all we had. But she would fix something. If my grandfather wants tortillas, she would make a little dough, just enough to make tortillas for the bunch there. She would pull out the hot coals and just throw her dough right on top of the hot coals to make the tortillas. They tasted good because they were fresh.

Then, as we traveled, there was one time when there was a Spanish man who was riding a donkey. I don't know where he was going, but he caught up with us. And the donkey was sort of lazy, taking a lazy walk, moving its head back and forth. As it moved its head, its lip just flapped together. My little brother was riding at that time in the wagon, and we were both looking out the wagon box watching the donkey. I said to my little brother, "That donkey is telling us a secret. Look at his mouth, he is trying to tell us something." So we watched, and his mouth was flapping: we did not know what he was talking about, just flapping his lips together.

Then, after watching it a while, that donkey stepped into a prairie dog hole by accident, and then he stumbled so the rider fell off. We thought that was funny. We should not have laughed, but we thought it was funny. And I told my little brother, "That is what he was trying to tell us! He did not like carrying a rider on his back, so he stumbled and made the man fall." But the man got up, he got his hat, dusted it off, put it back on, climbed back on the donkey, and rode on some more. Pretty soon, he took a side trail and went over on the other side of the hill, and he was gone. So, that is another little experience that we had on the road.

I was telling you about the tortillas. After tortillas are eaten, the supper eaten, it is time to go to bed. My grandmother always put our mattresses down on the floor, on the ground. (I say "floor" because we say "nangeh" inside for a floor and "nangeh" outside for the ground. So they are both called the same: nangeh. So, I get mixed up when I tell you in English. It is a floor inside and ground outside.) So she would put our mattress on the ground under a tree. The tree is for shelter in case it rained during the night. It would not hold much water you know if it rained, but that is what she told us it was for: shelter in case it rained.

I liked the firelight shining on the leaves, and I would lay there and watch the light on the leaves. Then there are stars up in the sky. Stars are beautiful to watch in the night time when you are sleeping out. I watched the stars before I went to sleep. And it is so pretty. Nature is really beautiful. You get to watch the stars; you get to breathe the fresh air; you feel the wind in your face as you go to sleep.

My grandfather never bothered to tell us stories on rides home, except when I asked him a question about the little bugs or the animals. One time when we were going, there was an ox in the field, and it was throwing dirt up, making mud and throwing dirt up. And I said to my grandfather, "Look! Why is that ox throwing dirt? There is nobody there for him to throw dirt at. He is just throwing dirt in the air." And he said, "He is trying to cool himself off. He has a temper. He got up with a temper today, so he is trying to cool himself off by throwing dirt around." Well, whatever he said was okay. I guess that is the way you cool yourself off when you have a temper: do something.

Anyway, we finally made it to San Juan Pueblo. I don't know how many nights we spent on the road, but it didn't matter: they were nice. It was nice to travel in a wagon all day long. If you get tired, you can crawl out of the wagon box and run along on the side. Sometimes you even run into the meadows. Not too far, but away from the road, and if you were getting left behind you can run. My grandfather never turned around to see if I'm in the wagon box or if I'm running back there, because his horses go slow enough that I can run and keep up. Sometimes I'm out of breath when I reached the wagon, and I would get back in the wagon box to recover. And I'm okay.

Well, we did make it to the village, and it was a different life from the life I was living with my mother and my dad. This was the Indian village at San Juan. All the grownups were responsible for children, so I not only had my grandfather and grandmother, I had all the elders in the village to care for me. It is a *good* feeling to have so many take care of children, but we in turn are their little errand messengers. If they want us to do an errand for them, they would tell us. We would go, take off, running, and do whatever errands they want us to do for them. Or, we just help around doing whatever they are doing. So it was nice growing up in the Indian village. We had many models to follow.

Coyote Tales on the Wagon Trail

Have you ever been to an Indian village? Things are different, a lot different now than they used to be. I grew up in San Juan Pueblo, at my grandparents' home. I have a mother and dad, but they were way out in Ute country. It is in Colorado. When my grandmother and grandfather came to visit in a covered wagon, I thought. . . . Well, when they were getting ready to leave, I did not think that the trip was going to be so long. I thought it was going to be a trip that they were taking for just half a day. And as a little girl, I was a tag-along. I tagged along wherever my father went, wherever my grandmother went. I was their tail.

When my grandmother and grandfather were getting ready to go back home, they had their covered wagon all ready and packed. My grandfather would put up a lot of hay on the bottom for his horses, just in case they stopped someplace where there was not enough to eat. And then their mattress went on top. So that was a very comfortable place to sit, in the wagon box. My grandfather drove, and my grandmother would sit in front with him, until she got tired. Then she would nap in back. Of course, I sat in back.

Children cannot sit still very long, and I was just a child. I would sit for a while, and then I would crawl down the back of the wagon and hang on to the wagon and run for a little while. Then, after a while, maybe I would see a little chipmunk running into the grass. And I stop and chase the chipmunk. Of course, that little chipmunk is much too fast for me.

Sometimes, it is just little bugs that try to get away from the roadside. There were a lot of stink bugs. Did you ever tap them on the back? Well, I did that one time. I was going to catch it, and so my finger tapped it on the back. Do you know what it did? It stood on its head, with its hind end up. This is protection for the stink bug. That is why they are called stink bugs. I did not smell it then. I just thought it was so funny to see that little bug stand on its head, with its hind end up.

"Coyote Tales on the Wagon Trail." Tape 12, told at the Reginald Chavez Elementary School, Albuquerque, June 17, 1998. Recorded by M. Ellien Carroll. Transcribed and edited by Tilar Mazzeo; edited by Sue-Ellen Jacobs, Henrietta M. Smith, and M. Ellien Carroll.

I told my grandfather about it, and my grandfather said, "Do you know what that little stink bug was doing?" I said, "No." He said, "That stink bug was listening to what was going on in the earth down below." And I asked him, "Who is he listening to?" He said, "There are people down there. They are saying 'Gather the fastest horses that you have and chase Coyote.'" Coyote seems to be always getting in the way. So they were going to round up all the coyotes and take them somewhere where they can be fenced up. There are always coyotes.

And coyotes are good. My people at Ohkay Owêengeh used to listen to the coyotes. Coyotes always tell them when there is a Spanish person coming. From which ever direction they are coming, the coyote tells them there is an enemy coming. And they hide the food. They hide what they raise in the garden. The Plains people used to come in the fall and steal their crop. And sometimes there is a child out where he is not supposed to be, and they will take the child with them—and will steal their women. So there's always that kind of problems at home. So Grandfather always told us about the coyotes.

Coyote also knows when it is going to rain, when it's going to snow. When it is going to be a big snowstorm, and it's going to be cold, the men go out to get wood, so they can be warm during the time it snows. That is what coyotes are good for. Nowadays, we do not understand the coyotes. We do not listen to them enough, although they still howl. They still make a lot of noise. They come and steal chickens, but then they have to survive. There are always stories about coyotes. So when my grandfather tells me things like that, I always believe. Sometimes, he tells me just to entertain me. I guess it's a good way to take care of the curiosity that children have. Because I'm like any other child—I ask too many questions, the "Why?" and "Where?" and "How come?" And those questions have to be answered.

He was a storyteller. A good storyteller. I learned most of my stories from my grandfather. So he has a chance to tell me a story about the stink bug. He did, he did. And children have imagination. There is that little TV that goes on up in your head, and you form your own pictures up there. Like I did then. I could imagine the people down below gathering their horses to chase Coyote. But, as I say, Coyote is good.

It was a time when there were no fences. Now, when you go anywhere, there are fences on both sides. There is a fence everywhere you go. At that time, the whole earth was free to travel wherever you want to go. And my grandfather traveled in a wagon, so he had to feed his horses. He always picked a place where there is plenty of grass to eat and water to drink for his horses. That means we stayed wherever night falls.

There were no motels along the way for people to sleep. You carried your bedding with you, and wherever night falls, that is your home for the night. My grandmother always picked a place where there is a tree, and she would build her fire right close by the tree and cook supper. Then she would sit with us and tell us a story. We just lay there. My little brother and I just lay there and looked at the stars. Stars are beautiful. You see them flying this way, shooting that way. And so we watch. We watch the stars. And the firelight on the trees, the trees moving around, it seemed like they are dancing—having their own dance. So watching that and hearing my grandmother tell a story, we just fall asleep.

So she goes to bed, but her bed is inside the wagon box. We never hear her crawling into the wagon box. After we go to sleep, we just do not hear anything, not even the coyote howl. So morning comes, and we smell the fire when she is going to cook breakfast. We get up, we get up to see what she is going to cook us for breakfast. Food always tastes so good out in the open. Like I said, there were no McDonalds, no hot dog stands, no potato chips. I'll bet you think it's awful, but it's not. There were no motels. You are all on your own, with just the horses and your grandpa, blue sky and nature out there. It was a beautiful way to travel and learn.

Okay, now we go to the village, and I will tell you about my growing-up days, and then you will get your animal story. So you have to wait like the coyote for your animal story. It might be a coyote story. We will see.

My First Time Living in a Tewa Village

When we got to the Pueblo in San Juan, that was my first time in a village. Living with my parents, we lived in a place where there were other people besides Natives. I think my father's family was the only Native family that lived in that town, because he was working for the school. My mother kept house.

It was during the First World War, and the soldiers were not supplied with some of the things that they have now. They were needing socks. When it was cold, they needed a hat—warm hats, warm mittens. So the Red Cross gathered as many women as they could and taught them how to knit. So my mother learned how to knit. And she helped knit mittens, warm mittens. She helped make socks and scarves.

I never learned how to knit. I asked her to teach me, but I suppose it was too much trouble teaching a little one how to knit. I just learned from her how to crochet. That is all I learned from her.

She would crochet, so I wanted to do the same thing, and I asked her to teach me how to crochet. She had a needle and spool of thread, and she said, "You learn how to make a turn." So I did that. And then, when I learned how to make a turn, I looked at her, and I said, "Now teach me how to make that pretty thing." And she said, "You have to learn more. Roll up your thing on there, and we will use that up to make something." Well, I never learned how. I think I went to San Juan Pueblo before I learned.

So, at San Juan, it was a different way of life. People lived in houses with another house right next door. The wall to the neighbor's house is also your house. All the rooms were facing together. So, my grandmother, when she wants to talk to her sister, who lives next door, she would just knock on the wall. And then my aunt would come to see what she wanted. Sometimes they would share a cup of coffee or a soda, a soda my grandmother bought.

"My First Time Living in a Tewa Village." Tape 9, told at the Van Buren Middle School, Albuquerque, March 1988. Recorded by M. Ellien Carroll. Transcribed and edited by Tilar Mazzeo; edited by Sue-Ellen Jacobs, Henrietta M. Smith, and M. Ellien Carroll.

Atole is boiled cornmeal. Take a pot of water, put your cornmeal in there, and stir it. And when it boils, it thickens. It thickens just enough—like cooked cereal, only it is a little more watery. That is what atole is. My grandmother always had atole, especially in the evening. A cup of hot atole will put you to sleep.

After supper, after we have done the dishes, we would be sitting on the floor or whatever. We always sat on the floor. We did not have chairs, and we did not have a table. We had mattresses, but not a bed. So, in the room, in the night time, when you go to bed, you just unrolled the mattress to put on the floor and the blankets that are folded on top of the mattress. You lay out the mattress, you put it on the floor, and you slept on the floor. Then, the next morning, when you get up, you just roll up the mattress against the wall and roll up the blankets and set them on top. And that is what you use for a chair if you want to sit down. And the children come running in, and go running out into the play area, in the village, in the plaza, where you can play.

My Stuffed Squirrel

We never had any toys. I had a puppy dog, and I had kittens. Those were my playmates. My little brother liked to play marbles. When we would go to the river banks, to help the man with his animals, we would pick up round rocks for my brother to use for marbles. Then, with a spool of thread, I would help him make a top with it. You cannot spin it the way you spin with a string; you just needed to spin it between your fingers. But he was happy with it. And there were always stick horses. My brother would cut himself a willow branch and leave the end part bushy, so that his horse has a bushy tail. And he would ride it. Then he would have a bow and arrow.

These were seasonal games. The men of the village would decide when it is time to put away the winter toys and bring out the spring and summer toys. And it was always that way. Little girls all had little stuffed squirrels to play with. I didn't have a stuffed squirrel because my grandfather was not a hunter. He did not go hunting. In fact, when we had a wild rabbit to eat in the house, it was not my grandfather who went hunting. We would go for wood to the hills, and then, if my grandfather would see a rabbit, he would tell my grandmother, "Get ready there is a rabbit coming your way." So she wore a shawl all the time. She would take her shawl off, and then my grandfather would chase that rabbit her way. She would stand there and just throw her shawl on the rabbit, and that rabbit would get tangled up. And that is how she caught the rabbit. So I say she is the hunter, not my grandfather.

I didn't have a stuffed squirrel, and all the girls had stuffed squirrels. When I want to play with their stuffed squirrels, I would borrow one from one of my friends. They would let me hold it just a little while. And then they will take it back, so I have to give it back because it is theirs. Then I will borrow from somebody else. And then I would play with it a little while, and, when she wants it, I have to give it back. So I went to my grandfather and told him, "I want a stuffed squirrel.

"My Stuffed Squirrel." Tape 4, told at STORYFIESTA™, Albuquerque, 1997. Recorded by M. Ellien Carroll. Transcribed and edited by Tilar Mazzeo; edited by Sue-Ellen Jacobs, Henrietta M. Smith, and M. Ellien Carroll.

All the girls have stuffed squirrels, and I don't have a stuffed squirrel." So I guess I pestered him long enough. One day, when my uncle was going for wood, he said to my uncle, "Bring us back a squirrel, bring us a squirrel so I can make a stuffed squirrel for my little girl." I felt good. This time I was going to have a stuffed squirrel.

He came home with a squirrel, and my grandfather skinned it. He just cut the leg part and pulled it off like an underwear. Then, around the eyes, he was real careful, and around the mouth. He left the ears there. Then he put it on a pole wrong-side out and put ashes on the skin, so that the flies would not bother it. He put it on places where the worms start, so there will not be any worms or flies. So that is how he put it on the post. And then, in a few days, it was dry. He brushed off the ashes, and he started working it until it got soft, soft enough to where he could stuff it.

When he was making it, I knew that he was going to finish it that day. So he stuffed it. My grandmother used to wear a red flannel skirt all the time under her top skirt, and she saved a bit of red flannel and gave it to my grandfather for the eyes and the mouth. That is how all the squirrels were made—with red eyes and a little red tongue hanging out. I sat there and watched him sewing.

He sewed even better than a woman, because he made moccasins for the women, and he made his own moccasins. With his own moccasins, he was not careful with the stitches—he just overcast. For the women, he used two sinews. He would start with one on top and one underneath. When he made his holes, he would put the top sinew through the hole and pull it down, then push the bottom sinew up through the same hole and pull it up. And he used real fine stitches. It looked beautiful, like a machine had stitched it. So I watched him sew it [the squirrel] around the eyes, around the mouth, and around the little red tongue. Then he sewed the cut that was there. He sewed that up.

It was already stuffed with wool. We had wool for stuffing pillows, and the wool was used to stuff the homemade mattresses. I think my grandmother pulled some wool out from one of the pillows to give to my grandfather to stuff my squirrel. When he finished it, he gave it to me and said, "Here, take your squirrel and go play, but you take care of it." I was going to take care of it, take good care of it, so I said, "Okay." So I went.

My friends were playing, and I showed them. I said, "I have a squirrel too." I said, "My grandfather made it for me." So I showed it to them. They looked at it. It is just like theirs. So I got it back, and I took that squirrel everywhere I went. When I went to take messages places or run errands, I took my squirrel with me. I did not have sense enough to leave it home, alone, when I had something to do. I took it with me.

And one day, my grandmother sent me on an errand to her sister's. Her sister lived up on top of the roof—up on top of the roof, where she had another little room. That's where she lived. She would move up there in the summertime. She said it was cooler up there than down here. So she was up there. I do not know what I went there for, but it was an errand.

So I took my little squirrel, and we had to climb ladders. They are not the steps like you have: they are the sticks, with a ladder, and they stood up sort of straight. So I had to climb that, and having my little squirrel I tried to put it under my arm and tried climbing it. Well, it worked all right, because I can pull myself up with one arm and hang on with the other one, while I pull myself up.

It worked all right going up, but coming down it did not. I tried different ways. I put my squirrel under my arm, but I could not go down—not the same way as I came up, pulling this way. So then I would get the squirrel, and I would put it under my neck. But it was too short. It did not fit right. Then I thought I would put it in my mouth and carry it down in my mouth, but it felt yucky because all that fur was still on it. So I took it out of my mouth, and I did not know what to do with it; I did not want to leave it up there.

So I looked down, and there was my little puppy. My puppy was still a playmate, but I think my puppy was jealous of that stuffed squirrel that I had, because I never played with the puppy anymore after I got my squirrel. But he was still waiting for me down there, wagging his tail, looking up at me, waiting for me to come down and play. I thought, "Well, that is my puppy. He is my friend. He has always been my friend." So I got my squirrel, and I threw it down there.

The puppy grabbed it and ran around the house. I came down just as fast as I could and went chasing the puppy. But I never found it. I lost my squirrel. I don't know what he did with it. I found the puppy; the puppy was there. He came home in the evening. I looked for the squirrel, but I never did find him. And so I never pestered my grandfather for another squirrel. I was supposed to take care of it, and I didn't: I lost it. So, that is the end of my squirrel.

We saw one when we went to Navajo country—to Cherrytown. I was telling them that story and a little boy sitting there listening to it just got up, just got up and said, "Wait! Wait, I want to show you something!" So he ran home and came back with a stuffed squirrel. Just the same as mine! Red eyes and a red tongue, and the tuft of hair up there. His grandmother made him one. So, it was not just my people who made squirrels. His grandmother made him that squirrel. But they do not make them much any more. Now it is store-bought stuffed animals, store-bought toys. And I don't even think they play with bows and arrows.

Native Values and a San Juan Childhood

It does not matter what generation you grow up in. Your childhood is always a happy childhood. At least mine was. Many a time now, I think about my childhood, and I wish that all children had the kind of a childhood that I had. My people were all responsible. The elders were all responsible for children's welfare. They all took care of us. They took care of children, and they took care of the older people.

The old-age people who stayed in the village in their own little homes were cared for by the folks who were able to work. Somebody would go and gather their dirty clothes and take them home and wash and dry them. We did not have to worry about ironing them. They just shook them and hung them up so the wind took care of the wrinkles. And when they get them down, they would brush them nice and fold them up again to take back to the old people. So they had clean clothes to wear.

If somebody close by cooked, they would always cook extra, so they could take them something to eat. So the older people didn't have to cook. It is what we have now at our senior centers. They feed us. They give us warm meals so that we can have something to eat. But, of course they don't wash our clothes. The younger people clean house for them, wash clothes, and cook for them. Sometimes, when the men go for wood, they chop enough wood to take to the old people.

Of course, older people didn't stay together in one place. They stayed in their little homes that they had when they were first married, I suppose. They grew old in their own little homes, and that is where they stayed. They didn't have to go to old-age homes. There were no old-age homes. The community took care of the elders, as well as the young ones.

In the early days, children were used for messengers. Any time anybody making bread wanted to send maybe a piece of warm bread

"Native Values and a San Juan Childhood." Tape 10, told to Native American Librarians at the New Mexico Library Association Roundtable, Santa Fe, May 19, 1998. Recorded by M. Ellien Carroll. Transcribed and edited by Tilar Mazzeo; edited by Sue-Ellen Jacobs, Henrietta M. Smith, and M. Ellien Carroll.

to somebody, or a loaf of warm bread, they would call us and say, "Take this to so and so, on the other side." So we would take the bread and run, take it to wherever they told us to take it. That was our job, and we did it willingly.

We were also taught to respect our elders. My grandfather always told us to respect our elders and he also showed us respect. If he was thirsty, he would ask for water. And then my little brother or I would take the water in a gourd dipper if he was thirsty. I would take it to him, and my grandmother would tell me, "Stand there, and make rabbit arms. Make rabbit arms." So I would stand there with my arms folded across my stomach until he is through drinking water. Then, when he is through drinking water, he would give me the gourd back, and I would take it away. That was a sign of respect. You wait until he is through drinking. So they had their ways of teaching by doing. That is something that I think we are overlooking now. We do not teach our children respect, respecting the elders, respecting our neighbors, respecting our friends, respecting ourselves.

Sometimes, when I look back and see the old folks as they work. . . . Certain days, certain times of the year, like now, people will be cleaning the ditch. The men go to clean the ditch. The women on one side of the village, the side where the governor lives, will take the lunch to the men first. And then the next day, it is the other side's turn to take lunch. The children were asked to help. It was fun to be excused from school on certain days, just to help. So, we would carry our little buckets, or sometime it's just a little water pail.

My grandmother had a basket, and in her basket she had either tortillas or maybe fried bread. If she was not lazy, she would make fried bread. And sometimes it was oven-baked bread. She would put her bread around her basket and in the middle maybe a pot of chili or a pot of beans. And then that tied-up basket would go on top of her head. They knew how to carry their baskets. I think if we did more of the things that our elders did, we would not be so sloppy walking around. My grandmother had such a perfect posture, just like carrying water, carrying her load on her head. She stood up straight.

Food and Sharing

Growing up in the village, I had my grandmother and grandfather to take care of me. But I also had all the grownups, all the adults who were able to work and do things. They were there for children. For all children. So we were lucky. We had many models to follow.

And we were taught the values of the village. We were taught the values of the Tewa world. And it was not a place where we sit down and have to listen. They modeled what they were teaching us. That was a nice way to learn.

When my little brother was with me, I had to trick him into coming to the village, because I needed a playmate in the house. I had playmates out in the village. I could play with other children. But when it is time to come home, and I went home, I just had my grandmother and grandfather. And they cannot tumble around with you on the floor and play like children. They were getting old in their years, so I needed a playmate. And I tricked my little brother into coming to the village with me. He was homesick at first, but I helped take care of him. I made him bows and arrows. I taught him how to shoot bows and arrows. That is in the fall. Children had seasonal games. They had things they played with in the summertime, they had things they played with in the fall, they had things they played with in the wintertime, and during autumn. So everything was seasonal.

So we learned a lot from my people. The old people were able to stay in their own homes and grow old gracefully, without leaving their homes. They were cared for just like we were being cared for by the elders who were able to work. There would be somebody who went to sweep their house and then cook their meal, wash their clothes. And that was nice. They had it made too.

It seems like all the things that my people did for the old folks are some of the things they are doing now at the senior centers. Except travel. The senior center has travel, where they can take them where

"Food and Sharing." Tape 12, told at the Reginald Chavez Elementary School, Albuquerque, June 17, 1998. Recorded by M. Ellien Carroll. Transcribed and edited by Tilar Mazzeo; edited by Sue-Ellen Jacobs, Henrietta M. Smith, and M. Ellien Carroll.

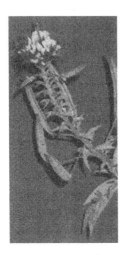

Figure 14. Bee weed, 1998. (Sue-Ellen Jacobs)

they want to go. But the old folks didn't have to leave home. There was always somebody who did that for them.

Maybe they wanted fresh vegetables. A lot of times my people would go out to the hills and gather some of the food that grows out there, it is just wild. We have the wild spinach, we have three different kinds of spinach. There is asparagus that grows along the river banks. And there is bee weed.

Bee weed is the first greens that we eat. Only you have to know how to cook it to make it taste good. And you pick them when they are just about so high [gestures, thumb to little finger indicating about 6 inches]. When they get to be about that high [gestures, over 6 inches] they are bitter. They are bitter when they are this high [gestures, over 6 inches]. So when you boil them, you have to keep changing the water, changing the water. About maybe five or six times, before the bitterness goes away. Then, after that, the fifth or sixth boiling, then you get all of the greens out of the skillet and fry onions, and mix it with the greens. Those are the best-tasting greens that I have ever had. The bee weed. They have purple flowers. When you are passing by and they have purple flowers, you smell them. And they do not smell so nice. But the hummingbirds like to build their nests on the bee weed stalks. They grow about so high [gesture, indicating between knee and hip, 2½ to 3 feet] and the little hummingbirds are small, they have little tiny nests. So they like the bee weed to build their nests.

And then there is whąą. I think that comes after the bee weed is grown, and it is not good to eat any more. Then whąą, then what do you call this other one . . . What do they call it in Spanish? Quellita [spinach]. That is gathered.

And my people shared. Whatever they had, they shared. I remember my grandmother used to go and pick the bee weed. She knew where there was a lot of bee weed, and she would bring a whole bundle on her back. She carried her load on her back, like a little donkey. And then she would lay it out. When she takes it home, she would lay it out and put a big shawl out there. And then she would lay the greens there, so the little ants that came along with the greens will have a chance to go off, and they will not be boiled with the greens.

Then, when she has the greens out like that, people passing by would say, "Mmmm. Where did you find that?" And then she would say, "Take some home, and fix yourself a good meal." And they would. You tell them to take them, and they take them. So that was sharing. She would take only what she needed, and the rest she gave away. And the older folks who were not able to gather their own greens, they had some of it. The people in the village make sure that they always had whatever was fixed in the home.

Work and Sharing

My grandmother was old, and she made pottery. She would roast chili in the outside oven. We have beehive ovens. They are built like half ovals with an opening here and a little hole on the top. We would build a fire in there. When the oven was hot enough, you would get all the ashes out and then put the bread in there and close it up at front. But up top, where the hole is, you do not close it right away. If your oven is all right, you close it in front and leave that top hole open, and then after awhile you look at your bread; if it is coming along good, then that is still kept open. But if it is not browning, then you stick something in the hole to cover it up, and then that browns the bread up. Oven bread is crusty. But it is good.

The oven is used for making bread, and then we also use it to roast piñons. When people go piñon-picking, they bring back a lot in those big seed bags, and you can roast a whole sack in the oven. Throw the nuts in there. Then you have something like a paddle that you use to get the bread out, and you use that to stir the piñons.

When you could hear the piñons that are in there popping, Grandmother would say, "Crack this piñon for me, and let me see if it is done." She would try one out just as practice. So I would crack it and show her the inside; if it were just a golden brown then it was done, so she would take them out. And we had piñons for all winter and some to share with those who did not go piñon-picking. That is a lot of piñons for just a little family to eat all winter, so she would share.

My people shared. They not only shared

Figure 15. San Juan Pueblo oven with fire, 1980. (Sue-Ellen Jacobs)

"Work and Sharing." Tape 4, told at STORYFIESTA™, Albuquerque, 1997. Recorded by M. Ellien Carroll. Transcribed and edited by Tilar Mazzeo; edited by Sue-Ellen Jacobs, Henrietta M. Smith, and M. Ellien Carroll.

Figure 16. San Juan Pueblo oven bread and pies, 1991. (Sue-Ellen Jacobs)

food, they shared work. My grandmother would put away her wash-ing—she might be doing the washing, while a neighbor or somebody would be plastering the outside of their house. At San Juan Pueblo it is the women who plaster the houses; in Santa Clara Pueblo, just a little way from there, the men plaster the houses. The woman's job is on the inside, but that is the way it was. The women at San Juan are good at plastering too. They did not use any tools to put the mud on the houses. They used their hands and would leave their fingerprints on the out-side walls, and that was good. So Grandmother would go help, because she was good doing it. Sometimes it would be a young girl who would

Figure 17. Piñon nuts before roasting, 1998. (Sue-Ellen Jacobs)

be trying to plaster her house, and she did not know yet how to do it, so Grandmother would go to help and show her. Sometimes it was somebody's floor that needed a plaster job, a new layer of mud floor.

See, we did not have the wood floor. We did not have the cement floors, or whatever other kinds of floors that you have. Ours was a dirt floor. The dirt floor does not last like the wood floors do, especially when we have the shoes like what are worn today. My grandmother would tell us, "You and your little brother are like horses when you come in here, you wear out a trail from the front door to the next room," and she always had to patch that up.

Growing Up with Respect

When I was a little girl, I was a tag-along. I guess you could say I was a tag-along when I was a little girl. I am still a tag-along. I tag along when my boys go fishing now. So I am still a tag-along.

Anyway, my grandfather and grandmother went to Ute country. That's where my dad was working, and they went to see him in the summertime. When they were getting ready to come back, I asked my grandmother if I could come back with her. And she let me. She told my mother that she needed a little girl in her house so that she would have somebody to send out on errands. That was my job.

All little children did that. We ran errands for different people, and all the grownups, all the adults, were responsible for the welfare of children. They helped take care of us. It was not just parents who took care of children. In my case, I lived with my grandmother and grandfather; but they were not the only ones to take care of us. All the adults were there, for all children.

And we had many elders who lived in the village, and they took care of the elders too, so that they didn't have to do without wood in the wintertime when it gets cold. Some of them could not go for wood, so it was up to the active people in the village to do that. They brought them wood and brought them food, washed their clothes, and cleaned their house. So even the old folks were taken care of, along with the children.

It was a good way to grow up. Children were taught the values of the Native people of our pueblo. We were taught how to respect ourselves, how to respect others, and to be polite and considerate in everything that we do. So there was a lot of love in the village, a lot of caring in the village. People helped one another, so that they got things done. If a person was sick in their house, he had plenty of help in the village.

My people did not ask for money, they just went willingly, volun-

"Growing Up with Respect." Tape 5, told at the San Juan Pueblo Church for visiting students from Los Alamos High School, March 1998. Recorded by M. Ellien Carroll. Transcribed and edited by Tilar Mazzeo; edited by Sue-Ellen Jacobs, Henrietta M. Smith, and M. Ellien Carroll.

teered, and did whatever work that had to be done. And it got done, because there was a lot of visiting and talking as they worked. Sometimes we get a silly person there, someone who would tease them. There is a lot of laughter when there is one like that around, teasing.

Caring across the Generations

My name Blue Water was given by my father. All of us have Indian names. The English names and the Spanish names we have, that we use in the classroom, were given to us by the Spanish people who came to our villages a long time ago. Because they do not have the sounds that we have, they had trouble saying it. We have a lot of places that are still supposedly being named in the Native way, but, because they cannot say it right, they say things like Chimayo instead of Tsimayoe.[1] That is one of the names. There are a lot of little places: Pojoaque instead of P'osuwäge.[2] So, see, it changes, because there are sounds that you do not have in English.

They gave our folks names, Spanish names—I suppose their own last names. The last names differ from one village to another, and after they run out of the Trujillos, the Garcias, and the Aquinos, then there were still a lot of them left who would have to be named. So they would say: "The rest of you are all Martinez." We have a lot of Martinez.

In my Indian way, you do not have last names. I am Blue Water, and that is all. I have no last name. And I suppose you wonder how people can find me or my family or anybody else like that. Well, now they go by their school name, not their Indian name. But I still go by my Indian name. At the village they call me Kó'ôe P'oe Tsä́wä́'. That is not all my name. Kó'ôe is an auntie.

In my village, we pass on the Native values. We teach our children all those things, so that when they get out from the pueblo, go out into the world, they still take that with them—all the values of the Tewa life and the Tewa way of thinking. And respect was one of the things. You have to respect yourself first, before you can respect your friends.

"Caring across the Generations." Tape 9, told at the Van Buren Middle School, Albuquerque, 1997. Recorded by M. Ellien Carroll. Transcribed and edited by Tilar Mazzeo; edited by Sue-Ellen Jacobs, Henrietta M. Smith, and M. Ellien Carroll.

1. When my people went trading their pottery (or whatever they had) they usually take bread, too. Coming home they may be tired, and they stop to rest. That is why Chimayo is called Tsimayoe. "Tsi" means "walking," "mayoe" means "being tired."

2. Pojoaque is a place where there was a little spring and people would stop there to drink water. It is called P'osuwäge because it is "water drinking place."

And that means—respect for one another means to love one another, have compassion for one another.

My pueblo always took care of children. Children maybe sometimes do not have parents. They lost their parents. But we do not have orphans. We have one who is left without a mother and a dad, but there is always a young couple who is waiting there to get the little one who is without a mother and a dad and to raise that little one.

My grandmother had many that she had raised. See, the reason why she was getting other people's children to raise was because she could not have any little ones herself. She always miscarried and did not have any little ones until my mother came along, and then she had a daughter. She had other people's children to raise. And for my mother, they were either her brothers or her sisters who lived in the same home with her. They were her brothers and sisters. So they are my uncles and aunts now.

And this is how it was, a long time ago. You come from a family, but you also have the whole village for a family. All the grown-ups were responsible for the welfare of the children, which meant all children had many grown-ups for models. And when you meet a person, you do not just pass them like a shadow going by, you always stop to say, "Hi Uncle. How are you this morning?" Or "Hello Sister, what are you going to do today?" And that is the way it was in the village. You are always greeting one another. It is still that way.

Sometimes I forget that I am not at the village. I meet people, and when they are passing by, especially when I am dressed like this [in her Native dress], they look at me and turn around. And I forget that I am not at home and say "Hi." A little "Hi" to somebody, treating them like you know them.

Meeting The Wizard of Oz *at Santa Fe Indian School*

Since you are all librarians, I think I will tell you all about my first experience here at the boarding school in Santa Fe. I was about ten years old when I was brought to the boarding school. I did not like the boarding school. I did not like being taken away from all that I was telling you about—the elders taking care of little ones and my grandmother's hot tortillas. We did not have fancy things, just beans, potatoes, and apples. But there was always a grandmother at home and always a grandfather there to tell you stories. And when you were hungry, your grandmother was always there. Then there were piñons.

Grandmother gave us piñons, but she limited our piñons. I guess if she let us have all the piñons we wanted, we would get sick! My little brother and I never seemed to get enough. We always wanted more. The more they gave us, the more we wanted. So Grandmother always made a little cone out of paper, about the size of her hand, and she would not fill it up. She would leave some room up on top, so it is just a little big.

"Sit outside, and eat your piñons," she would say. Which was good, because if we stayed inside with our piñons we would—well, I would hit him with a piñon shell, and he would hit back, and we would have piñon shells scattered on the floor in her house. And so she would tell us, "Sit outside, and eat your piñons, and watch people going by." So we would sit out there and eat our piñons, and, when we got through with our piñons, we would go inside and ask my grandmother for some more: "Mine is empty." "That's good," she said, "That's all you get. You don't get any more." So that's one thing I had at home that I left behind when I was taken to the boarding school.

Once you have finished fifth grade, then you are automatically taken to the boarding school. We had a whole room full. There was a

---

"Meeting *The Wizard of Oz* at Santa Fe Indian School." Tape 10, told to Native American Librarians at the New Mexico Library Association Roundtable, Santa Fe, 1998. Recorded by M. Ellien Carroll. Transcribed and edited by Tilar Mazzeo; edited by Sue-Ellen Jacobs, Henrietta M. Smith, and M. Ellien Carroll.

dormitory that was just full of new children, and because we were all homesick, you would see one crying. And the big girl who took care of us was not any help. When she saw us cry, she would say "Crybaby." We did not like to be called crybaby. So, when the tears started coming, we would get under our covers and cover up. Pretty soon, all the little ones are covered up, because they were all crying under their covers. They were homesick. But, after a while, I suppose we got used to it. We got used to it, and it was okay.

Going to school, we had one day of library. The lady who was there was quiet. I do not know if she did not have anybody to play with or talk to, and if that was the reason she was always quiet. She wore her glasses down here and looked at you over her glasses. Anyway, we would go to the library. I looked around. I guess the girls, the other children, knew how to pick out their books. They went around, picked out their books, and checked them out. But I was a dummy. I went, and I looked at every book. I think I was maybe just looking for pictures. I would get one book down, and if it did not have enough pictures, or if the pictures that I saw in there were not what I wanted, then I would put the book back. And I would get another one. Pretty soon, I'm the last one.

The librarian would come and say, "Did you find a book yet?" And I would say, "No." So she would come and help me. The first one she gave me was *The Wizard of Oz*. She said, "Here is a nice little book for a little girl to read." So, if she said it was a nice one to read, I took it. I took it to the building, and that night I opened it up. I wondered, "What is a wizard?" And then besides, I did not know how to read too well. And where was Kansas? The stories I heard are about little rabbits along the river bank where I live—locations that I knew where they were. I did not know where Kansas was, and I did not know what a wizard was. So, I just looked at it, and then I closed it up.

Next time, next week, when we went to the library, I gave it back to her. I do not think they were checking then to see who took out books or not. Mostly, we just put them back in there. And then I looked for another one. And always a dummy, I did not know how to look for a book. So I am the last one again, and then she said, "Did you find a book?" And I would shake my head. "Well, I will help you find a book," she would say. So she goes look, look, look. And she gave me *The Wizard of Oz* again. She did not know that I had already read it. There goes *The Wizard of Oz.* I do not know how many times I had that book. So that was my experience in the library.

Midwifery, Tewa Naming Traditions, and How I Got My Name

My grandmother's sister, older sister, was a midwife. And she would go and help some young mothers who are having their baby to deliver their baby. Many a time, she would go to the Spanish village and help them there. For payment, she did not get money. They gave her material. The Spanish people had no money, so they would give her material or pretty dishes. She had a lot of pretty dishes and serving bowls with flowers in the middle.

Because she was my grandmother's older sister and she could not work in the fields, her job was not only to help mothers but also to go around when people were sick. She would help take care of them. She got the medicine in the field, not in the stores. She knew what medicine was good for whatever is ailing a person. And so she would stay and help, and they might give her a pretty dish.

My grandmother's older sister, I forgot to tell you that she walks with a swaying motion, and she wore a shawl made out of a silk material that was given to her by the Spanish people. This material is always pretty, and it is like her when she walks—it sways back and forth.

She is the one who also gives the Indian name to babies when they are first born. We all have Indian names, and my Indian name means "Blue Water." I did not get my name from a midwife, but many a time I would go with the midwife to help her. Well, I was just a bodyguard. I was a little girl, and she would ask my grandmother if I could go to keep the dogs away from her. She was afraid of dogs, afraid the dogs might come and bite her. So my grandfather brought me a willow branch, so that I could put the dogs out of the way if any came at her. But nothing like that ever happened. No dogs ever came to chase her, and so after that I lost my stick. I did not take my stick with me, but I always walked in back of her.

"Midwifery, Tewa Naming Traditions, and How I Got My Name." Tape 6, told at the Rocky Mountain Storytelling Festival, Palmer Lake, Colo., August 7, 1998. Recorded by M. Ellien Carroll. Transcribed and edited by Tilar Mazzeo; edited by Sue-Ellen Jacobs, Henrietta M. Smith, and M. Ellien Carroll.

I thought she was walking with a dancing step. I always thought she was dancing when she walked. And when she carried the medicine in a pottery bowl, she always carried it up on her hand, near her head. For the newborn baby, she had two perfect ears of corn. By a perfect ear, I mean where the kernel is all formed to the very end. That is a perfect ear, and she always carried two. And because she walked with a swaying motion, she always carried the corn on the other side, with her hand on her hip. I always walked in back of her just to watch that little shawl swaying in the breeze. I thought she looked pretty—all the time as if she were dancing as she walked. That was the way she walked, with a swaying motion.

So I asked my grandmother, "Can I have a shawl just like my auntie? I want a shawl to wear when I go and help her." And so she made me one, but mine was a cotton shawl. And cotton is a little heavier than silk. Mine did not flutter in the breeze. But anyway, I wore mine. My grandmother would pin it over my shoulder, and pin it again to hold it. So when my aunt is walking, I look at her with the corn on one side, her hand on her hip and her bowl up in the other. So I would pretend I'm doing the same thing. I don't have anything to hold on this side, but she let me hold her corn. And I held the corn on my hip, and I walked with a swaying motion. I would look back to see if my shawl was fluttering like hers. Mine did not flutter, so I would go down more. I would bend down more to make it flutter. But it never did. And that is how we walked, from one end of the village to the other end, when she was going to name the baby.

And when we got to the baby, she would bathe the baby and dress it up with some of the clothes that she had made waiting the four days, for that little baby to get it. She always made little infant shirts with bright colors. One that I remember was a bright yellow shirt with red little flowers, tiny red flowers, and it had cuffs in front and up in back. And she would make some little flannel blanket, and she would wrap the baby up in the blanket, all the way down to the feet, including covering up the little hands. Then she would give the baby to me to hold, and the treat for being good was to guard her to all the way to wherever she is going.

I would sit there and watch the little baby's expressions. Newborn babies always make faces. They lay there. Sometimes they smile, sometimes they cry, sometimes they make crying faces, and then they open their eyes and just blink. And that is what I would look at. I would sit there and sit quietly and just hold that tiny baby while she gets the mamma ready. Then, when she is through, she will bring the baby back to the mother, and we all go outside.

Baby is going to be offered to Mother Nature and then given their name out there. So, when the baby is given to the mother, the midwife would have them turn a certain direction, and mother and baby would turn. So baby is offered to all six directions of the Native people. Our directions are not just north and south and east and west. We also have the above and below. So that is where the little one is offered—to all the directions of the Native people. Mother Nature is looking at a new-born baby, and that is how we get our names.

I was not so lucky to be offered to Mother Nature when I was born. My [Indian] name comes from my father.[1] My father was, at that time, a coal miner. He was way out in Colorado, working in the coal mines. My father only had a fifth-grade education, so he took whatever jobs he could get. And I guess a fifth-grade education was enough to be able to speak English. He also spoke Spanish. Well, one day I guess he had a day off, and he went fishing. When he went fishing, he had a favorite fishing hole. As he sat there, waiting to see if he could catch a fish, he thought about the fishing hole. It was just a little place. The water was deep and clear that day. And there was a blue sky, a blue sky that was reflected in the water, which made it seem even more blue. My father was not catching any fish. No luck. So he just sat and day-dreamed, looking at the water and daydreaming. And then he thought, "What a beautiful name that would make. Blue Water." So, when he went home, he said to my mother, "If we have another little girl, we will call her 'Blue Water.'" So, that is my name. I was the next little girl that came along. And that is how I got my name. Even though it is not offered to Mother Nature, I have a name from my father. He told me about it, and I treasure it.

---

1. This is a little note to explain about my other name, the Spanish name. I was born sickly and my parents thought I was going to die. So they took me to a little church, there in Utah where they lived. There was a priest and his housekeeper. They baptized me as Estefanita Ortiz, and that's what's on my birth certificate. But everybody called me "Esther" and I got "Martinez" when I married my husband.

Tewa Language and P'oe Tsą́wą́ʔ

When you call me by my Indian name, it is Blue Water. The adjective comes first and then the water—Blue Water. That is one thing they have in my language. In my language it is reversed. We say the water first and the color next. P'oe Tsą́wą́ʔ. P'oe is water. Tsą́wą́ʔ is blue.

When I taught in the bilingual class, we always went by our Tewa names. All the children who come to school have Tewa names, and if they did not have Tewa names I would give them a Tewa name. So when they come in the doorway, I would say "sengithamu" [good morning] whether it is a boy or a girl. So I called them by their names, and they would say "kóʔôe." Kóʔôe is auntie. This is one of the values that we have been taught—to greet one another, and not just say the name, but to make it personal. The person you are talking to is related—either an uncle or an aunt. So you say Aunt Blue Water.

Listen to my name in my language, listen to the beginning sound. P'oe Tsą́wą́ʔ. If you say it wrong, it is a pumpkin or a squash [poe]. And that was the mistake children were making. Sometimes they called me a blue squash. Or they mispronounce it and say P'oe Są́ʔwą́; then I would be a water squirrel! But that was nice. It did not matter what they called me. They were learning how to sound their words.

We have a lot of popping sounds. We have popping *P*, popping *K*, popping *T*, and then we have a popping *Ch*. The *Ch* pops and makes that sound. And the *Ch* is the sound at the beginning when you say "cheese." We also have tones that make a difference in meaning. A word may be spelled the same way, except tone, which makes a difference in meaning. I will say three words. I will say "water," I will say "moon," and I will say "road." "Water," "moon," and "road." You listen good, listen to the tone. "P'oe," "Póe," "P'ôe." Did you hear the tone? No? "P'oe," "Póe," "P'ôe." Did you hear them? The first one is low, the second one is high. "P'oe." "Póe." And this other one goes up

"Tewa Language and P'oe Tsą́wą́ʔ." Tape 5, told at the San Juan Pueblo Church for visiting students from Los Alamos High School, March 1998. Recorded by M. Ellien Carroll. Transcribed and edited by Tilar Mazzeo; edited by Sue-Ellen Jacobs, Henrietta M. Smith, and M. Ellien Carroll.

and then falls again. "P'òe." You have that tone in your language when you say "Ah, no." See? You hear it there, and you can make that sound. But we use the tone to show the differences.

If I were a stranger here and did not know how to talk your language, but I wanted a drink of water, I would come to you and say "khapo." Would you give me water? No, no, you would give me a rose. And if I said "P'oe," then I would get a cup of water. I would say "póe," and then I am asking for the moon.

PART 2

Thehtáy's Stories—As I Tell Them

Introduction

Storytelling Traditions at San Juan Pueblo

My stories are traditional stories. The stories I tell are all from my grandfather. When I was growing up as a little girl, we had storytelling on winter nights. Those were always the best times, because there were not only stories—there was also a big basket of roasted piñons. My grandmother would give us piñons in the house, but they were measured. She never gave us enough for us to get our fill of the piñons, because they always tasted so good. We never bothered to crack them. We just chewed them up, shells and all, so we could eat a lot more.

At storytelling time, no matter whose house it was, they always had a big basket of roasted piñons. I had a little brother who wore jeans, and he had two pockets. While the older people are listening to the stories, my grandmother would keep an eye on us. But sometimes she would get distracted. And then I would tell my little brother, "Your pocket is on this side. When Grandmother is not looking, you fill that pocket. Put in big handfuls in your pocket. This side is mine." So, when they are telling stories and when my grandmother is busy looking somewhere else, my little brother and I would take turns going to the basket. And we would get big handfuls and sit down. We behaved, because we had piñons in our hands. I would stick mine in his pocket on the right side, and his piñons always went on the left side. So we had plenty of piñons for the next day, when Grandmother does not give us any. That is part of the tradition of what happens at storytelling.[1]

"Storytelling Traditions at San Juan Pueblo." Tape 13, told at the Rocky Mountain Storytelling Festival, Palmer Lake, Colo., August 7, 1998. Recorded by M. Ellien Carroll. Transcribed and edited by Tilar Mazzeo; edited by Sue-Ellen Jacobs, Henrietta M. Smith, and M. Ellien Carroll.

1. I dictated these next paragraphs to my daughter so we could expand on the fact that stories are used in my Tewa traditions for teaching and for entertainment.

In storytelling there is generally a lesson to be learned. Sometimes it is survival as told in the "Hungry Coyote and Rabbit," or it may be for showing respect and kindness. This is obvious in "Old Man Bat and the Chickadees." In the story "Two White Corn Maidens and Gourd Boy" there are many lessons to learn: listen to your elders, respect them, and obey them; don't be lazy, do your share of work. If the two foolish young maidens had listened to their grandmother they would not have been distracted from their job by the good-looking young man with the sweet singing voice. In the story the boy who wears broken gourd earrings died some years past and was still roaming the village trying to find foolish people to take him home. He is known in the village as Pókhává e'nú which means "broken gourd boy" in English. He went about every evening singing his song to see if he could find foolish ones to take him home. The moral of the story is: Be careful who you bring home, don't bring home strangers.

In my grandparents' time storytelling was done for community socialization. Storytelling promoted teaching and entertainment and discouraged gossiping. A good storyteller always left you spellbound!

Animal Stories

Little Black Ants and Old Man Coyote

At San Juan Pueblo, behind the church, there lived some little black ants. They were very hard workers. They ground wheat for flour every day. One day, when they were grinding, Old Man Coyote was out hunting rabbits, and he heard them singing. He stopped in his tracks and stood with his ears standing up so he could listen. He turned this way, and he turned that way. He said, "Where is that beautiful music coming from?" He took off running in the direction where the singing sound was coming from. He found the little black ants behind the church. They were working very hard grinding their wheat. This is what they sang:[1]

Ants' Grinding Song

Esther Martinez

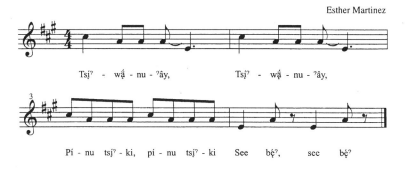

"Little Black Ants and Old Man Coyote." San Juan Pueblo Tewa Language Project CD-ROM v. 3.0, *Stories*. Recorded, transcribed, and edited by Sue-Ellen Jacobs; edited by Tilar Mazzeo, Henrietta M. Smith, and M. Ellien Carroll. A different version of this story is in the online audio files (no. 1), recorded in a private home at San Juan Pueblo in March 2002.

1. "Ugly little black ants, ugly little black ants / Pinched middle, pinched middle / Bent bellies, bent bellies" [English-language translation for versions 1 and 2].

Old Man Coyote peeped from behind the church and asked, "Little black ants, will you let me grind with you? I sure like that grinding song." The little black ants looked at him standing with his whiskers spread out. The little black ants were looking at Old Man Coyote. They were whispering, and one of them said, "Look at him, he has such big eyes." When he turned around to look at them with a smile, they saw his teeth. They were afraid of him but said to him, "Old Man Coyote, if you want to, you can sit there and grind, but first you will have to go and get the wheat. We are grinding wheat. We went to pick our wheat all this past week. We filled our little baskets." (They were using little acorn cups for baskets.) Old Man Coyote looked at their acorn cups filled with wheat. Then he asked, "Where am I going to put my wheat? I do not have a basket." They said to him, "You will have to look for one, maybe you will find something you can use. We are grinding wheat for flour, and we worked very hard all this week gathering wheat so we can not give you any of our wheat."

Figure 18. Black ant singing. (Peter Povijua, 1984)

Figure 19. Old Man Coyote. (Peter Povijua, 1984)

P'ósewhâa Sedó [Old Man Coyote] asked, "Where did you get that wheat?" One tsį́ʔwấ-nuʔây [little black ant] answered, "Over there at the threshing floor, where they thresh wheat. The Pueblo people are not stingy. They take a lot of wheat home to grind into flour, but they always leave plenty on the ground for us to pick, that is why we are grinding. Because winter is so long, and we do not want to starve—so we work hard during the summer days."

They pointed the way to the threshing place, and P'ósewhâa Sedó took off running. Just like a coyote, he had a long tail. He picked up his tail and used it for a broom to sweep up the wheat from the threshing floor. He was in too big of a hurry, so he had mostly sand and gravel mixed with a few [grains] of wheat. He gathered a big pile. He looked around to see if he could find something to put his wheat in, and he found an old rag that was thrown on the ground. He picked it up and put in the gravel mixed with wheat. He picked it up with his mouth and ran behind the church where the tsíʔwą́nuʔây were grinding. When he arrived there, he was so excited, because he had a big pile. Pʼósewhâa Sedó said to the tsíʔwą́nuʔây, "Look, I gathered a lot. When you finish grinding your wheat, I will give you some of mine. I have a lot."

When Pʼósewhâa Sedó put down his load, the tsíʔwą́nuʔây looked at one another, because he had a big pile of gravel and sand with a few wheat mixed with it. The tsíʔwą́nuʔây said, "It will be his flour that he will grind. It is not for us that he will grind. Let him chew rocks." They said, "Pʼósewhâa Sedó, there is room on that side for you to grind." There was a grinding stone where he sat. They were looking at the big claws he had and said, "How will he be able to hold the grinding stone with those big claws?" But they said, "If he wants to grind, let him learn." The tsíʔwą́nuʔây finished grinding, and they turned to Pʼóse- whâa Sedó: "Now it is your turn to grind your wheat, we will watch you to see if you will grind your wheat just as good as we did." He sang the same song that he heard the tsíʔwą́nuʔây sing. But he did not have a good singing voice. Because of the many bones he chewed, his sing- ing did not sound so pretty, like the tsíʔwą́nuʔây. This is what he sang:

Coyote's Grinding Song

Esther Martinez

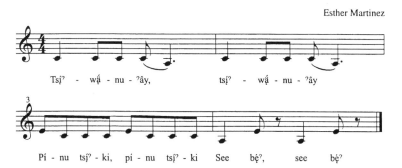

Tsíʔ - wą́ - nu - ʔây, tsíʔ - wą́ - nu - ʔây

Pí - nu tsíʔ - ki, pi - nu tsíʔ - ki See bę́ʔ, see bę́ʔ

The little black ants snickered when P'ósewhâa Sedó sang. "He is not a little black ant," said the tsí'wą́nu'áy. "He is P'ósewhâa Sedó, so why is he singing our song? He does not even look like a tsí'wą́nu'áy," they said, still snickering. One of the tsí'wą́nu'áy said, "He sure sings awful. I do not like his singing." The other tsí'wą́nu'áy said, "I do not like his singing either, but we will grind one more time, and, when it is his turn to grind, we will all hide between the cracks. There are a lot of open cracks along here where we can get in and run away."

P'ósewhâa Sedó said to the tsí'wą́nu'áy, "Now it is your turn tsí'wą́nu'áy. You sing so pretty." So the little tsí'wą́nu'áy sat down to grind, and they sang:

Ants' Grinding Song

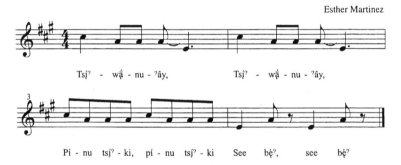

Esther Martinez

Then they said to P'ósewhâa Sedó, "Now it is your turn P'ósewhâa Sedó, now it is your turn to grind."

Then he piled his wheat mixed with sand, and he ground, sand and all. "Crack, crunch, crack, crunch" was the sound it made as he ground his sand. He had a few pieces of wheat, one here and there. But he was so proud. He had a big smile on his face as he looked around at the tsí'wą́nu'áy who were sitting around watching him grind his wheat. He was proud because now they let him grind, and he had learned how to grind. He started grinding his mixture of sand and wheat. He sang:

Coyote's Grinding Song

Esther Martinez

The tsį́ʔwą́nuʔây snickered. They thought it was so funny to see Pʼósewhâa Sedó sitting with his whiskers spread out and singing the tsį́ʔwą́nuʔây's song, and he did not even look like a tsį́ʔwą́nuʔây sitting there with his whiskers spread out. And, before he finished his song, the little black ants ran between the cracks to hide.

When Pʼósewhâa Sedó finished grinding what he had on his grinding stone, he looked around with a smile to tell the tsį́ʔwą́nuʔây how much he enjoyed grinding with them, but there was not a single tsį́ʔwą́nuʔây. He scratched here, he scratched there, he scratched all around that area until his claws started bleeding. He sat crying, then he went crying to White Sands, and that is where he lives now. The little blank ants are still grinding behind the church. Haheyinḑaʔmannamu. This is how long the story is.

Hungry Coyote and Rabbit

There was once a little rabbit who lived along the banks of the Rio Grande, and this little rabbit loved prickly pears.[1] He went out eating prickly pears. He liked best the red ones that are sweet—but they also have stickers, so do not try eating them without washing them off! This little rabbit loves prickly pear, and he also had those whiskers. He had little hairs around his mouth that will wipe off all the stickers, so when he eats prickly pear he does not get the stickers in his mouth. And Rabbit is a nibbler. He goes nibbling here and there. He will go find one nice, juicy, red pear and nibble at that one. Then, over there, he sees another one, and he will go nibble on that one, just nibble. And this little rabbit was having fun just nibbling on prickly pears.

But somewhere out in the wheat or in the trees along the river bank is Coyote. Coyote is tracking Rabbit. He sees the tracks, and he sniffs them. Coyote loves rabbits, and he is always hungry. He smells each little track that smells like a rabbit. And his mouth is just watering. Every little track he smells, his mouth gets more watery and hungry.

Finally, Coyote catches up with Rabbit, and Rabbit is on the look out for Coyote. He hears the branches rustling way over there, and he looks, there are those coyote ears. They are sticking out, looking for Rabbit. Rabbit sneaks over to the cliff. There was a cliff close by. He stood there, he said, "This is where Coyote is going to find me. Coy-

---

"Hungry Coyote and Rabbit." Tape 12, told at the Reginald Chavez Elementary School, Albuquerque, June 17, 1998. Recorded by M. Ellien Carroll. Transcribed and edited by Tilar Mazzeo; edited by Sue-Ellen Jacobs, Henrietta M. Smith, and M. Ellien Carroll.

1. When telling this story to an audience, I look to see if there are people I know there who I can use to include in the next part of the story. In a previously published version of the story (Martinez 1992), Coyote goes to the village of San Juan. There he first sees a woman outside making tortillas. He asks her if she has seen Rabbit. The woman answers, "No, I have not seen him. I have been busy making tortillas." Next Coyote sees an older man chopping wood. He says, "Thehtáy" (which is Tewa for grandfather), "have you seen Rabbit?" Grandfather says, "No I have not seen him. I have been busy chopping wood this morning." Next Coyote sees Enúkáy, a little boy, and asks, "Enúkáy, have you seen Rabbit." Well, the little boy started laughing, and laughing because Coyote looked so funny without any hair, but still he said amidst his laughing, "No, I didn't see Rabbit because I was digging worms so we could go fishing." With that Coyote went running to White Sands, where he still cries every night. If I know someone's name in the audience I will substitute their name for the "woman," "grandfather," or "little boy." It just makes it a little more fun for everyone.

Figure 20. Coyote sees Rabbit eating cactus near San Juan Pueblo. (Josephine Binford, 2002)

ote wants to eat me, but I am going to play a trick on him." So Rabbit stood there, and he is pretending to hold that cliff up.

Pretty soon, Coyote came sniffing. He smelt the last little footprint, and, like always, his mouth got really juicy and watery because that track smelled like rabbit. He looked up. There was Rabbit, standing up holding up a cliff. And he said, "Yummm. A tasty little rabbit. I have been chasing you all over the place. I have been tracking you and have finally caught up with you." And Rabbit looked at him, and he said, "But Coyote, you cannot eat me now. You see this cliff? Look up," Rabbit said. And there was a little cloud floating by, and sometimes when the clouds are moving and you stand under a tall tree or a tall building, you might think that the building is going to come down on you. That is what Little Rabbit was seeing. And Rabbit told Coyote, "Look at the cliff. This cliff is going to fall." So Coyote looked, and, sure enough, the little white clouds were passing by, and it did look like the cliff was going to fall.

So Rabbit said, "If you eat me, Coyote, you are not going to get much of anything. I am just a big bundle of fur. You are going to get a mouthful of hair. But I know where they are butchering a cow. I will bring you lots of meat." And so, Coyote said, "Okay. Okay, go get me the meat." The little rabbit said, "But you have to stand here and hold this, or it is going to squash both of us if I let it go." And Coyote said, "Okay, but you hurry back." So Coyote stood there, and, every once in a while, he looked. It looked like the cliff is coming down, so he really pushed. He is pushing hard all the time Rabbit was gone. And Rabbit was not looking for meat. He just took off. After a while, Coyote's arms got tired, because he was really pushing. And he said to himself, "What am I going to do? If I stand here, this thing is going to fall on me, and I will get crushed."

Pretty soon, I guess his brain started working, and he said, "I know, I will take three big jumps, and maybe I will not get squashed." So he gave that cliff a hard push, and then he jumped and jumped. And then he took another jump. And he looked back. That cliff was still standing there. And he said, "That darned little rabbit played a trick on me. This time, wherever I catch him, I am going to eat him up." And so he went chasing Rabbit, he went chasing.

And Rabbit was down by the river now. That Rabbit gets around. It was almost sunset, and there was half of a moon up in the sky. Rabbit said, "This is a good place to wait for that greedy old coyote. I will stand here and wait." So there was a pool there, and the moon shone its reflection in the water. So Rabbit stood there and waited. And pretty soon, Rabbit heard branches breaking down a little ways. And he looked. Sure enough, there was Coyote coming. His mouth was just foaming, because he was angry that rabbit had played a trick on him. And Rabbit said, "Oh boy. He sure is angry this time." "I do not think I have a chance," Rabbit thought.

Coyote came up and said, "You darned little rabbit, you played a trick on me. I will never be able to run any more. Just look at my arms, they are so sore I can barely walk." And Rabbit said, "I am sorry. But I was hungry a while ago, and there was a lady selling cheese. I bought some. I bought a big piece like that, and I cut it in half. I ate this half, and this half I saved for you, because I know you are hungry. I even put it down in the water so it will not get spoiled." And Coyote looked down into the water. Sure enough, there was a piece of cheese down there. And he said, "But how am I going to get that cheese? I cannot swim." And Rabbit said, "You do not have to swim. I will help you get it out. I will go look for a big cottonwood leaf, and then, when I find a big cottonwood leaf, I will bring it and put it on the water. And when I put it on the water, you can step on it and reach for the cheese."

So Coyote stood there, and Rabbit went looking. Rabbit found a leaf. And he said, "Coyote, I found a big leaf. You can get your cheese now." So he laid it down on the water. Coyote stepped on the leaf, and he reached down to get his cheese. But the current took him down the river, and he splashed. He splashed. He tried to get himself out, but there was no one around. He called for the green frogs to get him out, but the green frogs were nowhere in sight. So he splashed, and he splashed. And he floated down to the fork in the two rivers, where the Chama River is flowing into the Rio Grande. Just where they meet, Coyote was lucky that there was a willow branch hanging over. He grabbed hold of that willow branch, and he pulled himself up. He pulled himself up. Because he was so tired, he just laid down on the warm sand and went to sleep.

Pretty soon, one of the green frogs climbed up there and saw Coyote sleeping. And the frog said, "Look. Coyote is dead. I think he is dead." And then he went over there and pulled his whiskers. Coyote was so tired he did not even feel those whiskers being pulled. And the frog said, "Yes, he looks dead." Frog went around the other side of Coyote and pulled the whiskers on that side. Coyote did not even open his eyes. So Frog said, "Come, all of you. But bring your scissors. We are going to give that coyote a hair cut." So the green frogs started clipping Coyote's hair. They clipped, clipped, clipped, from the tip of his ears to the tip of his tail. They clipped him and clipped him. Coyote was there fast asleep.

After a while, Coyote got up. He stretched. He shook himself just like a wet dog shakes itself to get the water out of its fur. As Coyote shook himself, his hair started falling off! He shook some more. More hair fell off. And there he is, with no hair. And he looked. There was a pile of hair down there. "What happened?" Coyote wondered. He looked. Someone had clipped him! So that's what happened to Coyote.

Lazy Coyote and Mrs. Turkey

Coyotes like to go hunting, as you have already heard. But this story is about one lazy coyote. He hunts, but he never brings home any deer. One day, Mrs. Coyote said to him, "Today, if you do not bring anything for us to eat, do not bother coming home."

This day there was snow on the ground, snow where you could see the tracks of little animals. And Coyote went out, saying to himself, "What shall I do? I have no place to go. I have to go home." He went out, and pretty soon he found a cedar tree. He was passing by the cedar tree, so he sat down. And just then he saw Mrs. Turkey coming down the road, hurrying down the road. And he said, "My luck! I did not have to go out to hunt. I will just sit here and catch her."

So when she is coming by, Mrs. Turkey said, "Good morning Mr. Coyote. What are you doing sitting here so early in the morning?" He said, "Oh, I came to hunt, but I got tired, so I sat down." Then Mrs. Turkey said, "Do not bother hunting, because I am tired lately. I have been living too long, and I am tired. So I was just going to your house to have Mrs. Coyote cook me for your meal." And he said, "Well, okay then, I will just wait here until sunset, and then I will go home and eat." So he did not bother hunting. He sat there.

And Mrs. Turkey went straight down to the Coyotes' home and knocked on the door. And Mrs. Coyote peeked out and said, "Good morning Mrs. Turkey." Mrs. Turkey said, "Coyote sent me down. And he said for you to cook a bunch of sinew that he has hanging on the vegas [exposed ceiling beams made from tree trunks]." And Mrs. Coyote said, "That old man, that crazy old man, what does he want me to cook his sinews for? He is supposed to be out hunting." But Mrs. Turkey said, "I do not know. He just told me for you to cook the sinews." And then Mrs. Turkey flew off, so she made tracks in the snow just to Coyote's door.

About sunset, Coyote woke up and said, "I am so hungry. I can

"Lazy Coyote and Mrs. Turkey." Tape 13, told at the Rocky Mountain Storytelling Festival, Palmer Lake, Colo., August 7, 1998. Recorded by M. Ellien Carroll. Transcribed and edited by Tilar Mazzeo; edited by Sue-Ellen Jacobs, Henrietta M. Smith, and M. Ellien Carroll. This written version is slightly different from the audio version (no. 2) in the online audio files.

almost taste that turkey. She must be done by now. I will just go home and have me a good meal." So Coyote got up and trotted home. He trotted home, and he saw the tracks of the turkey go straight to the Coyotes' home. He saw the last footprint. He looked around, and it did not go any other place. That was the last footprint Mrs. Turkey made. So he said, "She did go in there. She did go in there. So I can have turkey to eat." So he went in there, and he said, "You better hurry and feed me, because I am hungry." And so Mrs. Coyote said, "Well, sit down, I will feed you." And she brought the bowl of the sinews all piled up. Coyote sat there and tried eating it. It was so hard. He pulled it this way, and he pulled it that way. He could not even chew on it. And he said, "This must be an old bird. No wonder she was tired of living." And Mrs. Coyote said, "What do you mean an old bird?" He said, "Well, I met Mrs. Turkey along the way, and she says she was going to come to our house, and she was going to offer herself to be cooked for our supper." And Mrs. Coyote said, "You dumb old man, that turkey came to the door, and she said to cook the sinews you have hanging up on the vegas, so that is what I did. And you had better eat all of it." So Coyote did the best he could, pulling the sinew this way and that way and using up all his teeth. And that is also why Coyote runs around barefoot today—because he does not have any more sinew to make himself moccasins to wear!

Coyote and the Fireflies

We have another story about Coyote which is just a little one. You see, Coyote is such a nosy animal that he always wants to know what somebody else is doing.

One day, Old Grandmother Spider was moving. Just about that time Coyote came sniffing, sniffing at Grandmother Spider's house. Grandmother Spider had a big sack that she wanted to move up on top of the roof, and since she did not have anybody to help her, she said to Coyote, "Will you take this sack for me up on the roof?" Coyote said, "Sure. I will take it up for you." So, he got hold of it with his mouth, and he started climbing the ladder up to the roof.

Pueblo homes have flat roofs and ladders to climb up on. So Coyote is climbing on the ladder up to the roof. As he was going up, Coyote started wondering: "I wonder what Grandmother Spider has in this big sack?" Remember, Coyote is always hungry. And he is hungry now. His stomach is growling. So he figured there might be food in the sack. So, as he climbed, he bit hard into the sack and made a hole. The sack got undone and out flew the fireflies! Grandmother Spider was moving the fireflies from the bottom of her house up to the top of the roof. And now the fireflies took off in all directions. And that is where your stars are.

"Coyote and the Fireflies." Tape 14, told at the Broward County Main Library, Fort Lauderdale, Fla., May 3, 1992. Recorded by M. Ellien Carroll. Transcribed and edited by Tilar Mazzeo; edited by Sue-Ellen Jacobs, Henrietta M. Smith, and M. Ellien Carroll.

Grandmother Spider, Coyote, and the Stars

Once upon a time Grandmother Spider lived at San Juan Pueblo. She lived near an irrigation ditch and there were nights when the moon wasn't shining that she had a hard time seeing her way. She is also a hunter and when she set her traps in the evening she is afraid she might fall into the water and become a titídí [water spider]. So, it happened that somebody had brought her a bag of mica clay. When she saw the clay sitting outside her little house she peeped in to see what was in the bag and she saw a lot of glitter in the bag. And she thought, "This might be a good thing to scatter around. Maybe we'll get some stars. We do not have any stars in the sky." So she called all the animals that live along the river banks and the animals from the mountains. And the mole came running first because the mole always stays underground and is never in the sunlight and she was glad to get out to be in the sun. So, there was the mole, and then there was the silver fox, the black bear from the mountain, and the deer from the mountain came down. And then Old Man Coyote came, too. So when they came, the mole came running to Grandmother Spider and said, "Grandmother Spider, I can help you carry that sack wherever you want me to." And Grandmother Spider looked at the mole and said, "You have a nice wide back to put a sack on your back, but your legs are much too short. You'll never make it to the place where I want you to take this sack." Because she wanted the sack to be taken down south as far as she can go, as far as he can go. And so, that was out. And then Silver Fox came and said, "Grandmother Spider, I can help you. I like to run in the bushes, I run through the bushes all the time." And Grandmother Spider said to him, "If you run through the bushes you are just going to tear up the sack before it is ready to be scattered." And said, "You can't take it." And then she looked around and saw the deer. And the deer came and said, "Grandmother Spider, I can run fast. A lot of times the people, the men from San Juan Pueblo come to hunt deer but I outrun them when they are going to shoot me with their bow

"Grandmother Spider, Coyote, and the Stars." Recorded by Sue-Ellen Jacobs at a private home at San Juan Pueblo, September 28, 2000. Transcribed and edited by Kathryn R. Smith; edited by Sue-Ellen Jacobs (no. 3 in the online audio files).

and arrow. I take off fast and they have not caught up with me." And Grandmother Spider said, "You do have good legs for running, but your back is much too narrow." Then the bear came and said, "Grandmother Spider, I have a wide back, I can carry that bag for you easy." And Grandmother Spider looked at the black bear and he did have a wide back, but he also had big claws. And she said, "Your back is good and wide for a big heavy load, but I don't like the looks of your claws. You're going to tear up the bag before you get very far." And so, then, there was just Coyote. So Coyote stood up and said, "Grandmother Spider, I can take your bag for you. I can run fast. I go stealing chickens every night. I stole Kóʔôe Pʼoe Tsą́wą́ʔ's chickens. I stole and ate every one of them and she came after me with a stick and did not catch up with me." So Grandmother Spider said, "Well, we'll try you out." "But you better do a good job," she said to him. So she put that sack of mica on his back. The mica was tied up with a strip of the rawhide that was cut off a deerhide. And he was tied up tight. And she said, "Hold this in your mouth and hold it tight. Don't let it open and go just as far south as you can go." And the coyote said, "Okay." And so he took the bag and the knotted strip of deer hide in his mouth. And Grandmother Spider said, "Bite hard into that knot so it won't untie." And he was doing just that, was chewing it up, chewing it up, and running at the same time, running. But he didn't get very far. He was a hungry coyote. He is always thinking about food and this raw hide tasted like deer meat. So he thought, "I wonder if Grandmother Spider remembered to put lunch for me. I am sure she put something in there because she is going to make me run far and I need something to eat on the way." So thinking about food, he kept chewing on the raw hide and he cut it through and the bag fell. The bag of mica fell to the ground and it opened up and all the little glitter that was in there started flying up. And all Coyote was thinking of was the lunch that Grandmother Spider might have put in there. And he looked in there and stirred the dirt around. The more he stirred up, the more the glitter would come up. And he would try to grab hold of the glitter to put it back in there. And then he would dig some more for the lunch, and then more glitter came up. And they went up, up, up, up into the sky. And that is where they landed. And that is where we got our stars.

Mr. Coyote's Feast

This story is about Coyote. Poor Coyote always gets mistreated, but he always thinks he is so smart he can do most anything. One day, he was out in the hills hunting, and he heard somebody singing. He listened. He said, "I wonder, I wonder who's singing. Somebody must be having a fiesta. Maybe if I go over there they might have something good to eat and feed me too." So he started running in the direction where he heard the drums.

There was a bunch of prairie dogs. I guess they were just celebrating the fun of being alive. So there was one of them with a drum, beating the drum, and the rest of them were all in a circle singing. And he listened. "I have to go and learn that song too." So he came and he looked, and he sniffed, and he found the prairie dogs. They were all having fun. So he stopped, he said, "Can I play with you? Can I dance with you? I heard that singing, and I want to come join you. I want to dance with you." So they let him dance, and he stood there right in the middle with his big long nose.[1]

Prairie Dogs' Song

Esther Martinez

Ta - mú   ta - mú   tąą   phụ   phụ

Ta - mú   ta - mú   tąą   phụ   phụ

"Mr. Coyote's Feast." Tape 13, told at the Rocky Mountain Storytelling Festival, Palmer Lake, Colo., August 7, 1998. Recorded by M. Ellien Carroll. Transcribed and edited by Tilar Mazzeo; edited by Sue-Ellen Jacobs, Henrietta M. Smith, and M. Ellien Carroll (no. 4 in the online audio files).

1. "Little grass bags, / little grass bags. / We're nothing but grass, / we're nothing but grass."

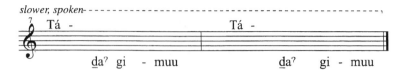

And the prairie dogs knew that he loves prairie dogs. He is always out hunting rabbits, prairie dogs, and quails. "Well, this day he was going to have a good load to take home"—he thought! So, as they danced, he joined in the dance. And then one by one, he would grab a prairie dog and he had a gunnysack to stick them in. He kept on dancing while they were singing. And then he'd grab another one and throw it in the sack. And pretty soon, he was the only one that was dancing. And he said, "I guess that's all of them. Now I'm gonna have a feast."

So he built a big fire, a big fire. When the fire turned to hot charcoal, he put all those little prairie dogs in the hot fire to roast them. And he said, "Umm, now I am going to have me a feast. I am going to eat all I can hold in my tummy, and take the rest to Mrs. Coyote. She'll

Figure 21. Coyote invites himself to prairie dog feast. (Josephine Binford, 2002)

be glad to get some of these." So. He put all the prairie dogs in the fire, I mean in the hot coals, and he had to wait awhile for them to cook, so he sat down.

And pretty soon, he started dozing off. He was watching, watching his goodies, but he went to sleep. And he was sound asleep when down the hill came two wolves, two grey wolves. And they said, "What is Coyote doing here sleeping by the fire?" They looked at him and said, "Hmmmm. Do you smell something? It smells delicious. Let's see what he has cooking in the hot coals." So they dug around, and they found the roasted prairie dogs. They were all cooked. And Coyote was sleeping, sound asleep. So they ate the prairie dogs. With their greasy hands, they went over to Coyote and greased his mouth up and greased his hands. And Coyote just slept. He slept.

Then the two wolves had finished Coyote's feast, they took off to the side to see what Coyote was going to do when he woke up. And after a while Coyote stood up, he stretched, and he said, "Oh, what do I have to eat. I think they are done. I can smell them." So he went over there [to his fire]. He pulled a little foot up. It came off. And he said,

Figure 22. Coyote dreams of cooked prairie dogs. (Josephine Binford, 2002)

"My, they are done good!" And he pulled another one up, and all he found were just feet sticking up in the hot coals! And the two wolves were watching him. Coyote said, "Somebody ate my prairie dogs, but I'll find out [who]."

And then the Grey Wolf came down, and he said, "What are you doing Mr. Coyote?" And Coyote said, "I roasted some prairie dogs, and I thought I was going to have a good feast, but somebody ate them." And the two wolves said to him, "Who could have eaten them when you have grease all over your mouth? You even have little pieces of meat around your mouth. And look at your hands, they are all greasy. You must have ate them and then went to sleep." And he said, "But I don't even feel full. I feel empty." And the wolves said, "Why don't you stand there by that pine tree and jump? If you can jump up high, then you are hungry. But if you can't jump, then you are full." So he stood by the pine tree, and he jumped. He went almost to the first branch. And he said, "I did not know I could jump that high. But I am not full at all. I am hungry." Then he stood again, and he jumped some more. This time he passed the second branch and almost hit the third branch and he came down, and the two were laughing and giggling because their tummies were full. And he kept looking at his hands. They were greasy. He touched his face. He was all greasy around the mouth. "But I didn't eat and I still feel hungry."

After a while, he got tired of jumping to see if he was full, and he went home and told Mrs. Coyote that he did find some prairie dogs. He did find some nice prairie dogs, and he even cooked them. "But I don't know what happened to them," he said. "But look at your hands," she said. "You must have eaten the prairie dogs. Your mouth is all greasy, and your hands are greasy too. So don't tell me those lies. Now go find me something to eat."

So he went out again. This time he was too hungry. He couldn't even see straight. He went staggering down the road, trying to find at least a quail to take to Mrs. Coyote.

Well, that's the end of the story. Because when you cook and go to sleep and don't watch your food, somebody else is going to come and eat it for you.

The Deer Story

A long time ago, there were a lot of deer on the mountains, and the young buck who took care of the herd up on the west side saw that it rained on the east side of the mountain a lot. It was toward fall when he realized that the grass was not going to last all winter, and he was worried about the old ones, who did not have good teeth to chew on twigs and the grass. And he worried about the little ones too, because if the mothers did not have the grass to eat, if they did not eat good, they would not have milk for their little ones. So one day he called his group together, and he told them, "I have been thinking that we should move to the east mountain, because I watch, and every evening it is raining over there. We did not get any rain, and we are not going to have enough food to survive this winter. We will be losing a lot of our young ones. We will be losing a lot of our old ones. I do not want that to happen." So the herd said, "Okay," and then the buck set a date for the move. He said, "I will give you four days to get ready."

This is the Native way. For anything important, you have to take four days to get ready. If a person is going hunting, he takes four days to see that his bow and arrows are working right and that he has enough arrows. So four days is the number of days that he uses for preparing for a hunt. So the deer are taking four days too, allowing the mothers and then the little ones to exercise their little legs to be able to make it across the mountain. The older ones were doing the same, because older deer are like people. They cannot run, and they cannot go as far as some of the younger ones can go. They needed exercise to be able to cover the distance to the east mountains.

"On the fourth day," the young buck told them, "we will leave here early in the morning, before the sun even comes up." Before dawn they were supposed to meet at a certain place, because they were going to

"The Deer Story." Tape 4, told at STORYFIESTA™, 1997. Recorded by M. Ellien Carroll. Transcribed and edited by Tilar Mazzeo; edited by Sue-Ellen Jacobs, Henrietta M. Smith, and M. Ellien Carroll. The version included in the online audio files (no. 5) was told in a private home at San Juan Pueblo in September 2002. The original recording of the text version lacked sufficie nt quality for duplication. In the online version, some aspects of the story have been changed to give greater cultural understanding.

pass the village of San Juan. "We have to go through there, and the men are hunters," he said. "If the men get up during the time we are passing by, they might be going hunting, and we would be easy prey for them to get us there, so we have to go early."

So the herd came early, real early, and he lined them up. All the young bucks were in front, and the older ones were in the middle, so they could walk if they got tired and not slow down the herd. The little ones liked to play, so they put all the little ones in back with big bucks to watch them, and that is how they went. Then he said, "Follow me, and I will lead you."

So the young buck who was the leader went ahead, and then there were the rest of the young bucks, with the older ones in the middle and the little ones way in back, keeping up with the herd. When they were coming down near the river, the young buck stopped. He heard something and his ears stood up. He was listening in all directions. And then he said, "Listen, I hear something." So they all stood with their ears up, trying to listen for where the sound was coming from, and the young buck said, "What do you think it is?" They did not know, but it was coming from the village of San Juan. The young buck told them, "Well, you will see. We might beat them, but we have to hurry to get through the village of San Juan." So they went, they kept walking.

Now just before you get to the pueblo, there is a little hill that you have to go up, and because it was a dirt road the leader buck stopped again, and he said, "Listen. What do you hear?" And the older ones said, "It sounds like a baby crying." He said, "Yes, it is a baby crying." So the young buck said, "Be very quiet. Do not step on pebbles, so the men will not wake up, or they will get up and find us going through the village." So he went on ahead, and the herd followed him, and there on the roadside was a tiny little baby all wrapped up. Just its little face was uncovered, and he was lying there, moving around. The young buck stopped, and he said, "It is a boy baby! What shall we do with it?" And the older ones in the middle said, "Take him with us. We will raise that baby, and someday he will grow up, and he can be our shepherd, he can take care of us. He will know where to find the grass, so we will not have to suffer." And so, the young buck said, "I have big horns. I will lower my head, and you put the baby between my horns, and we will go from here." So, he lowered his head, and they put the baby between his horns. Because the baby was crying, the deer sang a deer lullaby so the little one would go back to sleep:[1]

Deer's Lullaby

Esther Martinez

Á   na - ví má - gé   má - gé   má -

gé - ây   Saʔ - yâ - a   ûn - whää - mú

sää   saa   Pîʔ - wên   nan - gú

hu - u   eʔ   eʔ   hu - u   eʔ   eʔ

And then the little one went to sleep again, so they hurried out of the village, and they went far into the hills. They got away without waking the men in the village of San Juan Pueblo. They got away good.

Now it was getting toward winter. The men in the village would always go for wood to bring for the elders and for the whole community. They would also bring wood to the kiva where they have their meetings. So it was their first day to go for wood, and there was this War Chief who took a group to gather wood. While they were gathering

---

1. "My little fawn, little fawn, little fawn. / Your grandmother has wild greens cooking for you. / You are coming along with us" (sound of deer stepping, softly, so as not to awaken baby).

wood, one of the workers stood up, maybe to wipe the sweat out of his eyes. When he opened his eyes, he saw dust coming down the hill. He sat there and looked, and it looked like something was coming down. The War Chief always stands guard out in the open to see if anything is wrong or if anything is coming, but since they were all helping the War Chief, he stood there and said, "Look. What could that be? There is dust that is coming down that hill." And they watched. It was a long line of dust, and as they were watching, the line of dust came a little closer. They saw that it was an Indian man who was leading the deer.

He had his hair hanging down, pretty black hair. This young boy had grown up fast, because he was fed animal milk. He grew like a little animal. He grew up fast. In no time at all he was running, and that was why he grew up so fast. It was him coming down that hill, leading the deer. He wore a quiver in back with his arrows. He carried on one side a cedar bow, and on this other side he had evergreen branches. As he motioned to the deer to follow, they came down the hill.

The War Chief said, "Look, somebody is leading a bunch of deer. All of you hide behind cedar bushes. We do not want them to see us. We are just going to look. Do not bother making any more wood." So they all found cedar bushes to hide in, and they were looking.

The young man brought the deer right between them. There were a bunch of men hiding on one side and a bunch of men hiding on the other side, and the deers' trail went right in the middle. They looked at him; he was a handsome young guy. He had on a buckskin shirt with fringes that hung down. His shirt was decorated with porcupine quills on both sides, and he had buckskin leggings that had a long braided fringe with a decoration of porcupine quills. On the side of his moccasins, he had a fan of red-tail hawk feathers, stuck into his shoe on both sides.

As the deer came and he led them, he waved that evergreen branch toward them, and they followed, followed, followed. He was taking them to a place where there was lots of grass. So they all passed. There was a lot of them: the young bucks in front, the older ones in the middle, and the little ones behind. There were a lot of little ones.

After they had gotten out of the way, the War Chief told his men, "Let us go. Just take with you what wood you have now. Let us go back and tell the Chief what we have seen." So they went back, and they called a meeting at the kiva. All the men went, and they asked the elders, "What shall we do? What shall we do?" And they told them, "Well, you get ready for four days, and on the fourth day you go up again and catch the young man in the buckskin and bring him to San Juan." They said, "You do not have to bring wood this time, just go there and catch the young man in the buckskin."

So the men went after the young man. They watched and watched, and pretty soon they saw the dust coming down the hill again, and they said, "Here he comes." So the War Chief assigned two strong boys on one side, and two strong ones on the other side, and one man to go with him. He ordered those four strong boys to catch that young man when he gave the signal. When the deer-man was coming right in front of them, he told them to get ready to jump and grab him, to hold him tight, and then to tie him up and bring him to San Juan.

So as the herd and the deer-man came down, the men were all hiding behind the hill. Their eyes were ready to pop out. He was such a nice-looking man, dressed in a buckskin and with long black hair down to his waist. In his hair he wore an eagle-feather plume, the fluffy kind. When he came in front of the four boys who were supposed to catch him, they all jumped at the same time, and one of them grabbed him. They tied him up with yucca rope, which they used to use back then. They put him over the donkey they took with them, and they took him to the kiva where the men were waiting.

They brought him to the kiva, but he was not talking. So the War Chief and his helpers were told, "You watch him for four days and make sure that there is somebody in the kiva with him every minute of the day. You are supposed to keep the fire going in the fireplace, do not let the fire go out." So the Chief had his turn the first night. Everything went fine. He had the fire going all night there in the kiva. He did not go to sleep, he just watched the young man in the buckskin. The next day another one of his helpers came, and this one did fine: he stayed awake all night and kept the fire going. It was the same way the third night. But on the fourth night they had a young one watching.

There was a young one who was helping, and he was a little foolish. They told him, "You be sure to take a nap during the day, so you will not get sleepy tonight when it is your turn to watch that young man in the buckskin." And he said, "Okay, you do not have to worry about me, I stay out all night long, and then I come home and work in the fields. I am used to it." But they told him, "You had better sleep, because this is important." And he said, "Okay." But he did not go to bed; he did not sleep at all during the daytime. He was out wherever he would be.

See, this is what he used to do in the night time when he did not have to wait in the kiva: he and his friends would go to the river, and they would do some gambling sticks. They would lower a fish net into the water and, after a while, they would pull it up. They might have one or two fishes. They would take those fishes out and put them in another place, and then they would lower it again. And they would sit and gamble. Then, at daybreak, they would divide up the fish and go back home. Then during the day he could get up and go to work, work in the fields, go for wood, or do whatever he had to do, and he would be alright.

This time he thought it was going to be the same. So he went, and he watched. He watched the young man sitting there in the buckskin, and he kept the fire going in the fireplace. But around three o'clock in the morning, his eyes started drooping, and then he would shake his head. He did not have sense enough to get up and walk around. He would just shake his head, and he still sat there. After a while, I guess, he went to sleep. He went to sleep.

When he woke up, the fire was out in the fireplace, and he panicked. He said, "I had better get that fire going. When they find out, they are really going to get after me." He took a pottery bowl and went up the ladder, which is what the pueblos have instead of a door. So he took his pottery bowl, climbed the ladder, went across the roof, and he stood there looking around at the houses to see where he could see smoke coming out. Just a little way away there was a house with a lot of smoke coming out. He said, "Gee, I am so lucky. I can just go over there and borrow some hot coals." So that is what he did: he went over there and borrowed some hot coals in the pottery bowl.

He was hurrying back to build the fire in the fireplace so the elders would not find out that he had fallen to sleep and had let the fire go out.

Figure 23. Deer dancers at San Juan Pueblo, 1992. (Sue-Ellen Jacobs)

As he was coming across the roof, inside the kiva he heard a rattling. He heard a lot of noise in there, and he stopped, "What is that? I just left one man in there, the man in the buckskin, and he was just sitting there." Then he came to the ladder, and he took one step down, and then whatever it was that was making all the noise just ran past him. When he looked, it was a buck, a young buck with big horns going across the roof, and that buck just jumped down and ran to the east side.

The young man went inside with his bowl of hot coals. He looked around. The young man in the buckskins was not there! He had turned into a deer and went back to his herd up in the steep hills.

So that is what happened. If the young one had stayed awake and kept the fire going and watched the young man in the buckskins, my people, my San Juan men, would be good deer hunters. But, because they did not watch carefully, they have to walk far, and maybe if they are lucky they might get one. That is the deer story.

Old Man Bat and the Chickadees, Version One

This story is about Old Man Bat and the chickadees. One time when the chickadees were learning how to fly, Old Man Bat was resting up in the steeple [of the church at San Juan Pueblo] and he heard the chickadees singing. He listened, and because he has never had any friends to play with he thought he might go down there and ask them if he could join them. So Old Man Bat came down and flew all over the Pueblo looking for the chickadees. He found them by the arroyo. They were all standing in line. The little chickadees were learning how to fly. Like little children who learn how to walk, the chickadees have to learn how to fly, and so they were practicing, and they all stood in line with their wings up, and they were singing:[1]

Chickadees' Flying Song

Esther Martinez

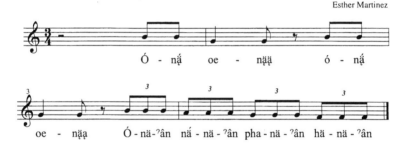

Ó - ná̧   oe - na̧a̧   ó - ná̧

oe - na̧a̧   Ó - nä-ʔân   ná̧ - nä - ʔân   pha - nä - ʔân   hä - nä - ʔân

They take off flying, and only two made it on the other side of the bank. The rest of them landed in the arroyo, where there was a lot of sand, and they laid there and laughed and laughed. When they stood up again they shook the sand out of their feathers and climbed back up on the arroyo.

"Old Man Bat and the Chickadees" (story version 1). From San Juan Pueblo Tewa Language Project CD-ROM v. 3.0, *Stories*, recorded, transcribed and edited by Sue-Ellen Jacobs, March 1996, for the San Juan Pueblo and University of Washington Tewa Language Project. Edited for this book by Sue-Ellen Jacobs, Henrietta M. Smith, and M. Ellien Carroll (no. 6 in the online audio files).

1. "Over on the other side, / over on the other side, / over there to that side, then back here to this side, / not quite over there / then over there."

Figure 24. Church at San Juan Pueblo. (Sue-Ellen Jacobs)

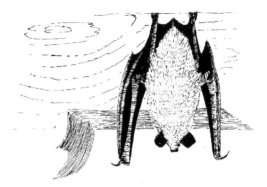

Figure 25. Old Man Bat. (Peter Povijua, 1971)

And just about that time, Síphêe Sedó, Old Man Bat, flew down from the steeple and he found the chickadees by the arroyo. And he asked them, "Chickadees, can I play with you?" The chickadees looked at him, and he didn't even look like a bird. They looked at him. He had a face like a mouse, and he had big ears. And he had fur instead of feathers. But they said, "You can play with us. You can play with us, Old Man Bat." And so Old Man Bat was so glad, he had found some friends for the first time.

And so they told him, "You go first!" And Old Man Bat said, "I heard that song but I don't know the song well enough, so if you'll sing, I'll stand and listen." The chickadees all got in line and spread their little wings, and they sang their song:

Chickadees' Flying Song

And they took off flying. Just three of them made it across, the rest of them were laughing so hard they got their feet all tangled up and

Figure 26. Chickadees.
(Peter Povijua, 1971)

landed in the arroyo where there was a lot of sand. And they laid there and laughed and laughed. And then when they got through laughing, they climbed back up on the arroyo. And they told Old Man Bat, "It's your turn!"

Old Man Bat stood up, and because it was the first time he ever had any friends, he stood up real proud and cleared his throat. He wanted to do everything right. And he stood there and he sang:[1]

Bat Sings the Chickadees' Flying Song

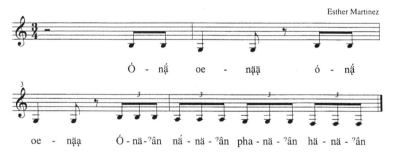

Esther Martinez

Ó - nä́   oe - nä́ä   ó - nä́

oe - nä́ä   Ó - nä-ʔân   nä́ - nä - ʔân   pha - nä - ʔân   hä - nä - ʔân

And he took off flying.

Old Man Bat knew how to fly. He flew all over the place, catching insects by night, and then he would rest in the daytime. So this is the first time he ever had any friends to play with, and he was so happy, and he laughed, and he just got his feet all tangled up and fell into the

---

1. "Over on the other side, / over on the other side, / over there to that side, then back here to this side, / not quite over there / then over there."

Figure 27. Síphêe Sedó
in arroyo, laughing.
(Peter Povijua, 1971)

arroyo. And he laid there and laughed and laughed. He laughed so hard that the tears were running down his face. And, then when he got through laughing, he got up and shook the sand out of his mouth, he took the sand out of his ears, and he climbed back up, and he told the chickadees, "It's so much fun playing with all of you. I never had any friends to play with." And he told them, "It's your turn, little chickadees. It's your turn to sing."

So the chickadees all stood in line with their wings spread out, and they sang:

Chickadees' Flying Song

Esther Martinez

Ó - ną́ oe - ną̈ą ó - ną́

oe - ną̈ą Ó - nä-ʔân ną́ - nä - ʔân pha - nä - ʔân hä - nä - ʔân

And they took off flying. And just two of them flew across. The rest of them just landed in the middle because they were laughing so hard. They didn't make it on the other side. And they laid there and laughed and rolled over and laughed some more, and they climbed back up on the arroyo bank. And they told him, "Síphêe Sedó, it's your turn!" And when they saw Síphêe Sedó sing his song, they whispered. "When he's singing this next time, we'll take off flying. He doesn't know how to sing. He sings awful, and he doesn't even look like a bird." Síphêe Sedó did not hear them whispering. He sang his song:

Bat Sings the Chickadees' Flying Song

And he was still laughing when he flew, he just got his feet all tangled up and landed in the arroyo. Síphêe Sedó knew how to fly, but it's the first time he ever had any friends, and he was so happy and laughing so hard that he got his feet tangled up and landed in the arroyo, and he laid there and laughed and laughed. And then he climbed back up on the arroyo. And there were no chickadees there waiting for him.

He looked around and he said, "Where are my friends? I was having so much fun. Where did they go?" And then he looked at himself, said, "I know. I know. I don't look like the chickadees. I do not have feathers, I just have big bat ears and a face like a mouse. That's why they took off." So he sang his sad little song, and his song only says, "I am a bird just like the chickadees, the only difference, I have mouse fur. I have the face of a mouse, and big ears, and bat wings."[2]

Bat's Song

2. "I used to be a bird / I used to be a bird / I am still a bird, / but I just have mouse fur, [then Bat makes his sound, which is] wée tsi²-tsi, wée tsi²-tsi."

Tsí - dé - bá   o - muu   wän

Naa - wá   O - pi - wîn - phó - muu   Gá

wée   tsi⁷ - tsi   wée   tsi⁷ - tsi

So he flew back up to the steeple, grabbed hold of the rafters and hung his head, and went back to sleep. So Síphêe Sedó, Old Man Bat, is still hanging up by his feet in the rafters, sleeping by day and working by night.

And we tell this to our little children so that they can be good to one another. We cannot do things that everybody else can do. Sometimes we cannot do the things other people can do. And we may look different. And when people make fun of you, you feel hurt, and sometimes you feel bad enough that you want to cry. So be good to one another.

Old Man Bat and the Chickadees, Version Two

Have you ever heard a story about a bat? Bat is a bird. The little bat is a worker, and he never had any friends. The little bat lived up in the steeple at San Juan, where the bell is, way up there in the steeple somewhere. And he hangs up there during the day. All day long, he would hang by his feet, his head hanging down. And he would sleep all day long. And then, about this time of day, he would get up and go fly out to catch insects—insects that harm the crop of Grandfather.

I always say "Grandfather," because in my family, when I was growing up, it was my grandfather who planted watermelons, and corn, and melons, and chili. I did not care for chili at that time, but now I do. I liked his watermelon and melons, and I loved his corn.

So, the little bat would fly around to catch insects, so that Grandfather's crop will grow and produce a lot. And one day, when he was hanging from the roof, he heard laughter, a lot of laughter. And this little bat never had a friend. He was one lonely little bat, who worked all night long by himself. He had nobody to play with. He worked. And then he is always tired. He sleeps all day long.

But this certain morning, I guess he came in kind of late. There was laughter outside, and he said, "I wonder who is having fun? I wonder if they will let me play with them if I went down there and if I ask." So Bat flew down from the steeple, and he went looking. He flew all around the village, looking to see where the laughter was coming from. And pretty soon, he saw some little chickadees.

The little chickadees were learning how to fly. Little birds have to learn how to fly, just like you learned how to sit up. When you were a baby, you learned how to stand up. And then, once you have got your

"Old Man Bat and the Chickadees" (story version 2). Tape 12, told at the Reginald Chavez Elementary School, Albuquerque, June 17, 1998. Recorded by M. Ellien Carroll. Transcribed and edited by Tilar Mazzeo; edited by Sue-Ellen Jacobs, Henrietta M. Smith, and M. Ellien Carroll. We are once again including several versions of a story because they were each told to different groups of people. Like many storytellers, I try to tell my story to my audience, that way the story is not always told exactly the same. This version was told to a live audience. The previous version is one of several I recorded to use on our San Juan Pueblo Tewa Language Project CD-ROM v. 3.0, *Stories*, where the story is told in Tewa and English text, audio, and video formats.

balance, you can take your first staggering steps. Pretty soon, you are running. Now you run all over the place. Well that is the same way with little chickadees: they have to learn how to use their wings to fly.

So there was a whole bunch of them on the edge of the arroyo. And they spread out their wings, and they sang. Their song only says, "Over on that side, over there. Back over on this side, and not quite on the other side." And so this little bat was out looking, and pretty soon he saw those little chickadees standing all in a line. Bat said, "Can I play with you, please? I never had any friends to play with, but your song sounded so nice. I was just going off to sleep, when I heard your singing. So I went looking for you all over the village, and then here you are. So can I play with you?" And they said, "Sure. You can play with us."

But there was one little chickadee who said to the others, "I do not want to play with him." He looked at the bat, and he saw his big ears, and he saw his funny mouth. "He does not look like a bird. Look at his ears. He has a face like a mouse," he said. And they elbowed him and said, "Be quiet. We will let him play a while, and if we do not like his singing, we will fly away."

So they told Bat, "You can play with us Síphêe Sedó." Síphêe Sedó is the bat. And ko?êe?ây are the little chickadees. So the ko?êe?ây told Síphêe Sedó, "You can play with us. But you go first. You sing first." And he said, "I heard that song, but I really do not know it good. Why don't you sing, and I will listen." So the little chickadees spread out their wings, and they sang:[1]

Chickadees' Flying Song

Esther Martinez

Ó - nå̃ oe - nå̃å̃ ó - nå̃

oe - nå̃å̃ Ó - nä-?ân nå̃ - nä - ?ân pha - nä - ?ân hä - nä - ?ân

---

1. "Over on the other side, / over on the other side, / over there to that side, then back here to this side, / not quite over there / then over there."

And they flew.

They were having so much fun that they just fell in the sand in the middle of the arroyo. There was a lot of sand. And only two of them made it to the other side. The rest of them lay there. They laughed and laughed and rolled over and over. It was so much fun to have such a big crowd to play with. And then, after a while, they got up. They shook the sand out of their feathers and got the sand out of their ears and climbed back up. And then they told Síphêe Sedó: "It is your turn, Síphêe Sedó."

And Síphêe Sedó was so proud that he had friends. For the first time, he had a lot of friends who were willing to play with him. So he stood up real proud, and he cleared his throat. And he started singing:[1]

Bat Sings the Chickadees' Flying Song

Síphêe Sedó is not a singing bird, but he tries. And even if he sounded funny, he sang. And he flew. Síphêe Sedó knew how to fly, because he flew all over the place catching insects every night. But this time he was having so much fun his feet just got tangled up, and he fell in the middle of the arroyo. He lay there and laughed and laughed and laughed. He laughed until the tears came running down his face. And then he got up. He shook the sand out of his fur and took the sand out of his big ears. And then he climbed back up there. And he said, "Oh, this is so much fun, koʔêeʔây. I am having so much fun. I do not think I want to sleep in the daytime any more. I am going to come and play with you every day."

---

1. "Over on the other side, / over on the other side, / over there to that side, then back here to this side, / not quite over there / then over there."

Well, the ko'ée'ây, they were just playing then, to learn how to fly, so they can fly like the rest of the chickadees. It was the chickadees' turn. So they sang their song:

Chickadees' Flying Song

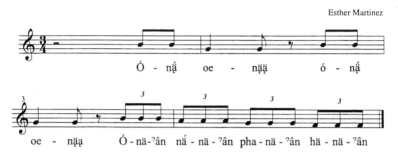

Esther Martinez

Ó - nä́   oe - nä̈ạ̈   ó - nä́

oe - nä̈ạ̈   Ó - nä-'ân   nä́ - nä - 'ân   pha - nä - 'ân   hä - nä - 'ân

And they flew. And most of them just landed in the middle, because they were laughing so hard. And they landed in the sand, and they rolled around, laughed and laughed. And then they climbed back up there, and they told Síphêe Sedó: "It is your turn Síphêe Sedó."

So Bat stood up again. He sang, and he sang. He was having so much fun:

Bat Sings the Chickadees' Flying Song

Esther Martinez

Ó - nä́   oe - nä̈ạ̈   ó - nä́

oe - nä̈ạ̈   Ó - nä-'ân   nä́ - nä - 'ân   pha - nä - 'ân   hä - nä - 'ân

And he took off, laughing. He was laughing so hard his feet just got tangled up, and he landed in the middle of the arroyo. He rolled around. He laughed and laughed. Then he got up, and he climbed back on the bank again.

He looked. He was standing all alone! I do not know where the little chickadees, the koʔêeʔây, had taken off. And he said, "Where did my friends go? I was having so much fun." Then he looked at himself: "I know. They do not like the way I look. I do not look like a bird at all. I have mouse fur, and I have big ears. And I have a face like a mouse and bat wings." So he sang his sad little song and flew up to the steeple again. And his song says, "I too am a bird, just like they are. The only difference is I have fur, and I have big ears. I have a face like a mouse, and I am a bat."[2]

Bat's Song

Esther Martinez

Tsí - dé - bá   o - muu   wän

Tsí - dé - bá   o - muu   wän

Naa - wá   O - pi - wîn - phó - muu   Gá

wée   tsiʔ - tsi   wée   tsiʔ - tsi

So he flew back to the steeple and grabbed hold of the rafters, hung his little head, closed his eyes, and went back to sleep. So now he does not have any friends any more.

---

2. "I used to be a bird / I used to be a bird / I am still a bird, / but I just have mouse fur, [then Bat makes his sound, which is] wée tsiʔ-tsi, wée tsiʔ-tsi."

We tell this to our children so that they can be good to one another. Not all of us can do the things that others can do. So, be good to one another, children, because it always hurts when you mistreat another one.

Old Man Bat and the Chickadees, Version Three

Although they are for children, when I tell stories on Thanksgiving, the grownups still turn their buttons, and they become children for these children's stories. My name is P'oe Tsą́wą́ʔ. I am giving you the sound of my Tewa name. P'oe Tsą́wą́ʔ. I was raised in my grandfather's house as a little girl, and what a great experience. You who have grandparents to talk to are so lucky, because I treasure my grandparents and the things that I have learned from them. My grandfather was a storyteller. Indian people got their lessons from stories they were told as children. So a lot of our stories are learning experiences.

When I was growing up in Grandmother's home, the whole community was responsible for children—their bringing up and their safety. They would make sure that children were not hungry. It is not just the parents who are responsible for children. The whole community was responsible for the respect that is taught to children. I work in the school, and I passed this on to children at the Day School. I believe children are our best resource. Someday they are going to grow up, and we are going to depend on our children.

Now we will have a story. I know the little ones like animal stories. These are stories that I learned from my grandfather. I am going to tell you about Bat. We have a bat, who is always up in the steeple of our church. He hangs upside-down, because that is the way bats hang. And he is the only bat around. The only bat. He has no friends, no neighbors—he is just the one lonely little bat. But close by are a lot of chickadees. Quite close to the school, there is the arroyo, and there are lot of chickadees there.

"Old Man Bat and the Chickadees" (story version 3). Tape 14, Florida, May 3, 1992. Recorded by M. Ellien Carroll. Transcribed and edited by Tilar Mazzeo; edited by Sue-Ellen Jacobs, Henrietta M. Smith, and M. Ellien Carroll. This version of the story was told to Youth Services Librarians and Educators at the Broward County Main Library in Fort Lauderdale, Florida. The previous version was told to elementary school children in Albuquerque.

On this day, the chickadees are jumping over the arroyo and back again, and they are singing:[1]

Chickadees' Flying Song

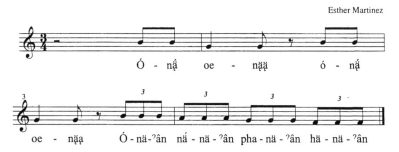

Esther Martinez

Ó - nā́ oe - nā̧ā̧ ó - nā́
oe - nā̧ā̧ Ó - nä-ʔân nā́ - nä - ʔân pha - nä - ʔân hä - nä - ʔân

And as they are singing, they would jump. Some of them are singing from the one side of the arroyo, others are singing in the middle of the arroyo, and some are flying to the other side. And sometimes they fall. So they get up, and they shake their feathers. They shake the dust out of their feathers and climb back on top of the bank again. They were having so much fun.

And lonely Bat was hanging upside-down in the steeple. "Perhaps I will lie here," he said. But then he looked around to see what he was hearing. Then he said, "I know, I will go and find out. It is such a happy sound." So Bat went down from the steeple, and he came down to where the chickadees were playing.

The Bat said to the chickadees, "Can I play with you? I want to learn the song too." The chickadees looked at him. He really did not look like a bird. He had big ears, funny looking wings, fur like a mouse, and his ears were like mouse ears. "Okay," so they said, "let's let him play."

So the Bat said to the chickadees, "You go first and sing, and I will listen." So the chickadees all got in a line on the bank of the arroyo, and they sang:

---

1. "Over on the other side, / over on the other side, / over there to that side, then back here to this side, / not quite over there / then over there."

Chickadees' Flying Song

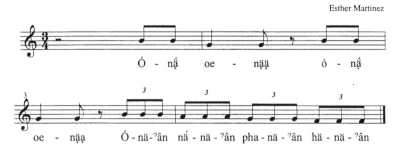

They jumped, and they sang their song. A lot of them landed in the arroyo, so they got up and shook the dust out of their wings. It was so much fun, because, when you are laughing, you do not quite make it to where you are trying to jump. It is always so much fun.

Then it was the bat's turn. "And now it is your turn, Mr. Bat," said the chickadees. And Bat said, "I know that song. I have heard it so many times." So Bat stood and stretched his wings. He held up his big, mousy ears, and he started singing:[1]

Bat Sings the Chickadees' Flying Song

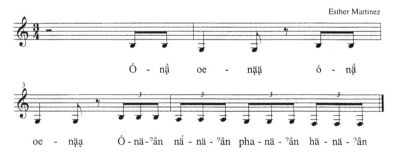

And the chickadees said, "Gosh, he sure sings funny." And they said, "Well, we will let him sing one more time. If we do not like the way he sings, we will take off."

---

1. "Over on the other side, / over on the other side, / over there to that side, then back here to this side, / not quite over there / then over there."

So it was the chickadees' turn. They sang and then flew over on the other side. Some of them landed in the dirt, but they were having so much fun. Then it was Old Man Bat's turn to play again. So when he started singing, he stood on the bank, and he was all ready. And the chickadees were sitting close by. They were going to take off. And when Mr. Bat started singing, the chickadees flew.

When Bat flew, he landed in the middle. Instead of going all the way across the arroyo, he landed in the dirt in the arroyo. So he got up and started laughing like a chickadee. He was having fun, because he had somebody to play with, after all those days hanging upside-down, day and night. Of course, he would get out in the night time to fly around, but he did not have any friends. During the day, he would hang up in the steeple, and overhear so much fun. Now, for the first time he had friends. And he could play with them.

But when he climbed back up on the arroyo, there was nobody there! The chickadees had flown away, and Old Man Bat looked around. He did not see anybody. He started to cry, because he did not have a friend to play with. He sat, and he cried. This was his song:[2]

Bat's Song

Esther Martinez

Tsí - dé - bá   o - muu   wän

Tsí - dé - bá   o - muu   wän

Naa - wá   O - pi - wîn - phó - muu   Gá

---

2. "I used to be a bird / I used to be a bird / I am still a bird, / but I just have mouse fur, [then Bat makes his sound, which is] wée tsiʔ-tsi, wée tsiʔ-tsi."

The Bat is saying, "I am also a bird, like the Chickadees. The only thing is, I have fur like a mouse." And "wée tsiʔ-tsi wée tsiʔ-tsi" [squeak squeak] is the sound that a mouse or rats make when they squeak.

So the Bat flew back into the steeple and hung upside-down in the steeple. And that is where he is still, hanging upside-down, because he does not have any friends.

See, when we are growing up and have to play with others, Children, we might be different, look a little different, and come from a different home. Maybe the color of the skin is different. But inside we are all children, aren't we?

So that is the lesson that our people would try to teach their children: no matter how different a person looks, you have to be a friend to that person.

Two White Corn Maidens and Gourd Boy, Version One

There once lived in San Juan two white corn maidens with their saʔyâa. Saʔyâa is the word for Grandmother in Tewa. The two white corn maidens are called white corn maidens because of their innocence and their youth. The white corn maidens ground corn everyday. This is customary in the Indian home. People ground corn so they can have something to eat during the day when they get hungry. And the two white corn maidens did the grinding, because Grandmother was too old, and she no longer ground corn.

One day, when the two white corn maidens were sitting at their ók'uḏa (which means the grinding stone), the grandmother said to them, "Hurry with the grinding so we can eat, because tomorrow you are going to pick some wild plums. We need the wild plums to dry for the winter so we can have something to cook during story time. We can eat the plums during storytelling time." So the two white corn maidens said "Okay." And when they got through grinding and had supper, they all got ready for bed.

Saʔyâa, because she is old and was tired, unrolled her whǫʔphąʔ— or mattress that you sleep on. She unrolled her whǫʔphąʔ and laid down and went to sleep. And when she was asleep, the white corn maidens undid their whǫʔphąʔ and got ready for bed.

The next morning, when they got up early, they went to pick the plums. And while they were picking, the younger maiden heard singing in the distance, which was coming their way. The younger one said to the older one, "Listen, I hear somebody singing." And the older one said, "It must be my nose you are hearing; my nose always whistles when I breathe." The younger one said, "Do not say that; listen, it is somebody singing."

So they listened, and sure enough there was singing. Somebody was

"Two White Corn Maidens and Gourd Boy" (story version 1). Tape 1. Recorded by M. Ellien Carroll in a private home at San Juan Pueblo, 1992. Transcribed and edited by Tilar Mazzeo; edited by Sue-Ellen Jacobs, Henrietta M. Smith, and M. Ellien Carroll (no. 7 in the online audio files).

Figure 28. White corn maidens grinding corn for their grandmother. (Peter Povijua, 1984)

Figure 29. The boy agrees to sing for two white corn maidens. (Peter Povijua, 1984)

singing, and the singing was coming their way. And so they hurried and picked their plums. When they were through, they waited for the singer to come by, and when he was passing by they noticed that he was a young good-looking boy. So they called him, and they noticed that he was wearing earrings made out of broken gourds. They called him and asked him to sing. They said, "Will you sing for us? You sing so beautifully." He stopped. And he said, "Yes, I will sing." And he sang for them.

The two girls said to one another, "Shall we take him home with us? Let us ask him to go home with us." And so they did. They said, "Will you come home with us? You can live with us; we live with our grandmother, but she does not have to know."

So they took him home, and they hid him in the storage bin where they store up the corn. And the grandmother scolded the girls because they were gone all day. She said, "Where have you been? I waited and waited. It should not have taken you so long to pick the plums." And she told them, "You had better fix something to eat so we can eat." The younger one made some atole; atole is cornmeal gruel that you can drink out of a bowl or cup. The older one made some posole. Posole is corn-meal stew. When they were through, the older one passed the posole, and the younger one filled up the bowls with atole. And they ate.

When they were through, because Grandmother was old and tired, she went to bed. She undid her bedroll [mattress], her whǫʔphą̨ʔ, and laid down for the night. She soon fell asleep. And when she fell asleep, the two girls went in to get the Pókhávi Eʔnú which means "Broken Gourd Boy." The Skeleton Boy has been roaming around to see who will pick him up to take him home. The two maidens did not know that they had brought home "Pénítʔaa Eʔnú" which is Tewa for "Skeleton Boy."

Figure 30. Finishing dinner. (Peter Povijua, 1984)

Figure 31. Skeleton Boy. (Peter Povijua, 1984)

They went in to get Pókhávi Eʔnú in the storage room, and brought him out, and told him to lay down in the middle and sleep. The two will sleep on the sides, on both sides of Pókhávi Eʔnú. So they went to sleep, and the next morning when Grandmother woke up, she went to get the girls up so they can go pick plums.

When she went to wake them up, she noticed that the skeleton boy was sleeping between the two of them. And she called the girls, "Wake up. Look who you have sleeping between the two of you." She grabbed Pénítʼaa Eʔnú by the arms and threw him out with a rattle. She threw him out in the yard. And the two girls got up and were wondering why Grandmother was calling "Gourd Boy," "Pénítʼaa Eʔnú" which means "Skeleton Boy," when they had brought home a nice-looking boy the night before. So they went out to look, and sure enough in the yard was Skeleton Boy, still wearing his gourd earrings.

The grandmother said, "You better be careful who you bring home. And I want you to let me know when you bring people home to spend the night." So when they saw Skeleton Boy out there, they were both frightened and promised their grandmother that they will be more careful and that when they bring home anybody they will let her know. And they promised that they will not bring home strangers.

Two White Corn Maidens and Gourd Boy, Version Two

Once upon a time, in the village of San Juan, there lived two white corn maidens with their grandmother. Every day the white corn maidens would grind corn, which was customary in the Indian homes. People grind their corn so they can have something to eat during the day. Most of the time it was atole or it was sahkéwe. Sahkéwe is a mush, a thick mush, that you can eat with soup poured over it. Atole is just a gruel that you can drink from a bowl or cup. The girls were young, and they were strong enough, so they did the grinding. The grandmother was old, and she did not grind anymore.

One day, when they were grinding, the grandmother said to them, "You had better hurry up with the grinding, so we can eat, because tomorrow you are going to go and pick some plums so we can dry them for winter. We need the plums to cook during storytelling time." So the girls ground the corn, and, when they were ready, they cooked supper. The big one had made some corn meal mush, which is sahkéwe; the younger one made atole. When it was ready, the older one passed the mush around so that everybody could have some. The younger one filled up the bowls with atole. When supper was done, they all got ready for bed.

Grandmother got them up early the next morning so they could go pick plums. As the girls were picking plums, the younger one heard someone singing out in the distance, coming their way. In these days, there was a skeleton boy who had died and who was still roaming around to see who he could find who was foolish enough to pick him up. He was called Pókhávi. Pókhávi means broken gourd, and he wore a broken gourd as earrings. That is why they called him Pókhávi. And he went about every evening, singing his song, to see if he could find foolish ones to take him home.

The younger girl heard the singing and said to her sister, "Listen, I

"Two White Corn Maidens and Gourd Boy" (story version 2). Tape 1. Recorded by M. Ellien Carroll in a private home at San Juan Pueblo, 1992. Transcribed and edited by Tilar Mazzeo; edited by Sue-Ellen Jacobs, Henrietta M. Smith, and M. Ellien Carroll.

hear somebody singing." And the older girl said, "It must be my nose you are hearing; my nose always whistles when I breathe." The younger one said, "Do not say that. It is somebody singing." They listened, and sure enough they heard somebody singing in the distance, coming their way. They picked their plums, and then they stopped and listened to see who was going to come by. As they were waiting, there was a young man going by with broken gourd earrings. Of course, they did not know that it was the boy who had died some years past and was still roaming, trying to find foolish people to take him home.

When he was passing by, they called out and said, "We heard you singing, and you sing so beautifully. Can you sing for us?" And he said, "Sure." So he stopped and sang. They liked his singing, so the two girls said, "Let us take him home with us. He can live with us." They asked him, "Do you want to come home with us? You can live with us. We live with our grandmother, but she does not have to know." So he went with them.

When they got to the house, they hid him in the storage room where the corn is kept, and they told him, "We will call you when it is time to go to bed." After supper, after they had cleared the dishes and when they were ready to go to bed, the grandmother, because she was old and tired, went to bed early. She unrolled her bed mattress and laid down to sleep. And when she had gone to sleep, the young girls unrolled their bedrolls, and they went in to get the gourd boy from the storage room. They brought him out and told him, "You can sleep in the middle, and we can both sleep on the sides." So they went to sleep.

The next morning the grandmother got up, and when she went to wake the girls up so they could go pick plums, she noticed that there in the middle was the gourd boy. So she called the girls and said, "Get up." She said, "You are supposed to go pick plums, and look who you have sleeping between you." She grabbed that gourd boy, who had turned to a skeleton during the night. She grabbed him by the arms and dragged him outside and threw him out. She got after the girls and said to them, "From now on you had better watch to see who you bring home. This one had been looking around to see if he could find any foolish ones to bring him home, and you have done that. So you be careful who you talk to and who you bring home. And do not be sneaking anyone into the house again. You let me know when you bring anybody home."

So the girls went out to see the gourd boy, because he was not a skeleton the day before. When they had brought him home he was a nice-looking boy. There, laying out in the yard, was a skeleton, still wearing the broken gourd earrings. They were both frightened and promised the grandmother that they would be more careful and would let her know when they wanted to bring somebody home with them to the house.

Sue-Ellen Jacobs, Esther Martinez, and Josephine Binford, 2002. (Walter BigBee)

Esther Martinez telling stories, 1992. (Naedin B. Martinez-Gallegos)

Storytelling, Headstart Program, Chamita, N.M., 1992. (Naedin B. Martinez-Gallegos)

Blue Water and a storyteller doll made by the potter Humming Bird from Cochiti Pueblo. (Josephine Binford)

The river at San Juan Pueblo where Esther Martinez played, 2001. She still goes fishing there. (Lynwood Brown)

Blue Water (left) with younger brother, Tony, and older sister, Virginia Heart, 1998. (Yvett Meely)

Esther Martinez's ninetieth birthday cake, with storyteller doll, May 2001.
(Lynwood Brown)

Opposite: Mother's Day gathering with family, May 2002. (Josephine
Binford)

Esther Martinez, explaining to students and guests the meaning of designs on traditional clothing. The photograph was taken when she was director of the Bilingual Education Program at the San Juan Pueblo Day School. (Bilingual staff)

Esther Martinez teaches her great-granddaughter, Celeste, about traditional ways in deer dancing, 2000, while Jordon Agoyo looks on. (Josephine
Binford)

Receiving congratulations from Ramón José Lopez on the occasion of receiving the New Mexico Governor's Art Award, 1998. Left to right: Josephine Binford, Esther Martinez (seated), and M. Ellien Carroll. (Adolphe Pierre-Louis)

At a storytelling fiesta in Albuquerque, early 1990s. Left to right: M. Ellien
Carroll, Esther Martinez, Henrietta Smith, Gioia Timpanelli, and Claire
Campbell. (Photo courtesy of Henrietta Smith)

AFTERWORD: MY MOM, MY BOSS
Josephine Binford (Ahkon Póvi)

In reading this book you have already met the Storyteller, Blue Water (P'oe Tsą́wą́ʔ). She is also introduced by her baptized name, Estefanita. Now I want to introduce you to our mother, our role model, and the grandmother of many. She is not only the grandmother of our children but also grandmother to all our friends' kids. All our friends and their kids refer to her as Saʔyaâ (Grandmother). Most of our friends are grandparents themselves now, and the grandkids and the great-grandchildren keep adding up. It is no wonder she cannot remember who is who. In our village and in the surrounding Tewa-speaking villages she is called Kóʔôe P'oe Tsą́wą́ʔ, or just Kóʔôe (Auntie). That is showing respect, respect for your elders.

My mother is one of two survivors of what were originally eight brothers and sisters. Her grandparents died when she was a young woman, she does not remember the year. Her grandmother died first, then about a year later her grandfather died. I am assuming her grandfather died in 1946 while I was a baby. Mother used to tell me stories of how her grandfather used to hold me on his lap. My great-grandfather used to sing to me, sometimes he would bounce me to the tune of his singing, then one day he dropped me. According to Mom, after that incident he was afraid to hold me. My great-grandfather lost his eyesight shortly after my great-grandmother died. My great-grandfather missed her so badly that he lost his spirit to live and even got head lice. Mother, being close to her grandfather, kept a close eye on him. One day, while taking a break from hoeing the garden, she came indoors to check on him, and she found him praying to the Lord. In his prayer he said, "Have mercy on me, oh Lord. I am an old man, an old man who cannot see, an old man who keeps bumping into walls. Lord,

I led a good life, a happy life; please, forgive me of my wrongs, have mercy on me; take me home, take me home." This was the last time my mother saw her grandfather alive, because he died about five minutes later. Many times we heard this story of mercy and miracle that the Lord bestowed on her dear beloved grandfather.

Life has not been easy for my mom, but she has made wise decisions in her life's journey. These decisions have made her life fun and colorful. Mother always looked at life's obstacles from a different point of view, many times with humor. For instance, when she was learning to read and write the Tewa language she was discouraged because she did not know what a verb or a noun was, nor did she know the other parts of speech. It had been over thirty years since Mother had last sat in a classroom. Anyway, she learned by making funny little sentences and working with an old Dick and Jane book. In her life she has had many roller-coaster rides. I will describe some of these adventures.

Mother and I were raised in the time of no electricity, no inside running water or inside toilet. It was a time when very few people had inside gas heating or had an automobile. I remember traveling by wagon to attend Santa Clara Pueblo's feast day on August 12 and going for wood in the wagon with my brothers and sisters. My mother was generally in the driver's seat; our wagon looked like the ones you see in the old cowboy movies today. Sometimes, when the horses were being used for other chores, we used to walk to the riverbank and carry the wood back in a large round tub that was also our bathtub. Yes, sometimes the load was heavy, but there were enough of us brothers and sisters that we took turns carrying the tub. And Mama was always nearby to give us positive feedback. I remember when my baby sister almost died from viral meningitis and everyone was lost for words. My sister was in the hospital, far from home and only my mother at her side. Where was her positive feedback? Supportive structure was plentiful within tribal boundaries, but outside of this it was limited due to cultural insensitivity. All the doctors told my mother that only a miracle would save my sister. My poor mother prayed and prayed. And guess what? A miracle occurred. My sister is alive.

In 1976 my second-eldest brother, Joe, was hospitalized in Las Vegas, Nevada. This was his second time in a coma related to alcoholism. According to the doctors, death was near. Again, my mother prayed and prayed. Three weeks later my brother came out of his coma, laughing. But his chronic problem with alcohol abuse had taken its toll. Now, his mental status was that of a toddler, and prospects for rehabilitation and relearning were dim. Nursing-home placement was highly recommended, but my mother refused. She brought him back to New Mexico by bus. My brother needed close monitoring; it was a period of confusion and chaos. Mother continued to work as a bilingual teacher. Although she wanted to quit her job, our family encouraged her to continue working, and we took turns helping with Joe's care. The brothers would take him for walks to the Rio Grande River or the Chama River. Sometimes they fished (actually, they more often untangled Joe's fishing line). But Mama believed in miracles, and she said that one day Joe would again go fishing or shopping by himself. And he did. How strong my mother's faith is. Many stories she told us have related to the work of God.

We had lived in the village, and we also lived with my grandmother across the Rio Grande—about two miles from the pueblo. Living near the river was fun; with money being scarce, Mother always made "quality time" for us by taking us to the river for little picnics. On the riverbank we would look for driftwood, and Mother always found pretty little pieces of it. She would talk to us about the beauty of that pretty little driftwood, its life, and how beautiful Mother Nature's artwork, her creations, are. She would then let us explore our own imaginations about how we would carve it.

My mother was the main caregiver for us, and she also provided for my grandmother's needs. My grandmother was also raising other grandkids, so my mother had extra mouths to feed. In those days my mother received welfare assistance of $93 a month; we were a total of ten brothers and sisters. She also took on jobs cleaning people's homes, and for extra money she would carve birds out of the driftwood we found on the riverbank. Selling the carved birds to tourists helped put food on the table. Sometimes she would trade them. One time, for example, a *Farmer's Almanac* salesman stopped by. My mother wanted the magazine but had no money. The salesman, however, admired her carved birds, so they made a deal. She gave him two carved birds, and he paid for two years' subscription to the magazine. My mother always looked forward to it arriving in the mail.

As a child, I also played jacks with rocks, and my brothers all had imaginary horses made with tree branches or twigs. We, too, had rolled-up mattresses that we used for chairs during the day, and when unrolled they were used for beds. During my childhood years, as with my mother's, people in the village grew their own food. As kids we were all expected to help in planting and in harvesting. No one was excused. Everyone worked together, from the youngest to the eldest. At harvest time we kids attending the Santa Fe Indian School were excused from school for about two weeks so we could help with harvesting. This was survival, and we worked hard in those two weeks. We picked corn after corn or chili after chili. Sometimes we would complain of working, especially when we got tired. But Mama always had an uplifting verse or comment for us. And that kept us going. More so when she promised to tell us a story that night. Most of the time we went to sleep before the story was finished because we were all tired from the day's work. Anyway, the elders say a Tewa person will never go hungry if he has corn; corn is the "giver of life" for our Pueblo people. May is corn-planting month (Khúų Ko Pʼoé), and it is also the month in which my mother was born.

Storytelling was also a fun time in our household when we were growing up and even nowadays. As adults we still love listening to Mom tell stories. Many times she has told us about her grandparents. She speaks with great admiration of both of them but more so for her grandfather. He used to call her his little princess. Every time my mother tells stories to us or to others, she makes the story come alive. She speaks in a low tone, with each word carefully and very gently spoken. When her words are spoken the words are treated like gold. We all sit very tentatively, listening to the story. Sometimes it appears as if we are under the spell of angel dust. We don't get piñions at our storytelling, we just sit there, mouths wide open, waiting for the next word to come out. These are fun times for us, our own quality time with Mama goes on.

Life has not been easy for my mother, but her strong faith and trust in the Lord have helped her through many rough times. After her mother died, she took a motherly role for the rest of her brothers and sisters, and then one by one they died, leaving only two of them. Her brother, whom she so fondly talks about in this book, died in 1981. As time went on, due to loss of loved ones, Mother's grief and sorrows became harder for her to deal with, especially every time she had to attend another funeral for one of her sons. Five of them have gone to their final resting place. I remember when the most recent death, that of my second-eldest brother, occurred in 1998, Mother was devastated. Within a week she had lost most of her eyesight. Before that she was able to read with the aid of a magnifying glass. Prior to losing her vision, she was able to do her transcriptions from tape and translations from Tewa to English. She would sit for hours under the porch or under the tree, doing her work. This was a horrible loss that she had to deal with.

Nowadays, Mom still sits under the porch or under the trees, but now she enjoys listening to the different whistle tones made by leaves blowing in the wind. Other times she is working on driftwood; carving birds is now done by touch. She no longer helps in planting and harvesting, but if her eyesight was better she would! On occasion, when the chili or the corn plants are large enough, she attempts to hoe. One time while hoeing she "mistook the chili plants for weeds," as she reminds us with her special humor and laughter. In the summertime, Mother stays outdoors as much as possible. She takes advantage of every opportunity to tag along on a fishing trip with my brothers or tag along with her grandson on errands, because she gets treated to an ice cream cone. At nights she wants to be outside so she can glimpse the stars with the little peripheral vision that she has left. Being out in the evening also gives her the opportunity to listen to the coyotes howling. And guess what we get? A coyote story or a story about the stars.

Mother continues to devote a lot of energy to trying to teach us to read and write the Tewa language. In the family, most of us speak Tewa, but we cannot write it. I am trying to learn to read and write the language, but it is not easy. When I do learn, this will be my "Ivy League" education, taught by the best scholar in Tewa linguistics.

My mother has shared with us her knowledge and the traditional values that she has learned from her grandparents. We, the sons, daughters, and grandchildren of Blue Water, know that our wówátsi (life) on Mother Earth is short. We were taught that life is a journey from the first breath of life to the last breath we take. Our journey will not be smooth; it will have rough spots and winding obstacles. What is important is which path (pʼóeʔą́ą̇) that we choose. She has encouraged us to choose a good path. That way we will always walk in harmony. Walking in harmony with Mother Earth will give us dignity, respect, and inner peace. And this will be a measure of our character. She has been our precious guardian angel when we went astray. There is so much we have learned from our mother. She has been a great role model. She has also been an ambassador for our village, sharing our cultural philosophies, beliefs, and values with people far and wide, both inside and outside our Tewa world, especially helping children learn about our ways. You have read how she does this through the stories in this book.

Now I have one more miracle story that I must share. On February 23, 2003, my Mom—my boss, as I refer to her—was hospitalized for pneumonia. While she was a patient at the Santa Fe Indian Hospital the pneumonia improved, but the day before discharge she had a heart attack that put her into heart failure. She was then transferred to Los Alamos Medical Center, where her condition deteriorated and she went into respiratory failure and then complete kidney failure. It was frightening, and we felt helpless. Now it was our turn to have faith and trust in God. We prayed and prayed. Mother was getting the best of care, and, like her, we believed in miracles. We contacted her friends by e-mail and by telephone and asked that they pray for her. And they did. On Friday, March 14, three priests from different local churches arrived at the hospital at the same time, said their prayers, and gave her the last rites. Within twenty-four hours another miracle had occurred: Her condition was reversed, and she was on her way to recovery. We thank all of her friends and our local community members for supporting us during that critical stage of Mother's life journey.

On March 18, 2003, she was discharged from the hospital and, as of this writing, is enjoying herself at home with the family. Now we treat her like a queen, not a princess. Her heart is not as strong as it used to be, but her spirit is. On her good days, we still get stories or quick Tewa lessons. She looks forward to warmer weather so she can go fishing.

It is impossible for me to describe the uniqueness of her individuality as a mother and as a grandmother in this brief reflection. I am happy that a grandson has expressed interest in writing a biography about her life. Right now, he is still working on his Ph.D. in Native American studies, and he gives credit to his grandmother for encouraging him and being his mentor.

EPILOGUE: REFLECTIONS ON P'OE TSÁ̜WÁ̜ʔ'S STORYTELLING AND THE MAKING OF THIS BOOK

Sue-Ellen Jacobs, M. Ellien Carroll,
and Henrietta M. Smith

P'oe Tsá̜wá̜ʔ has received many awards for her dedicated work to save her Native language, Upper Rio Grande Tewa, San Juan Pueblo dialect. The Woman of the Year Award from the National Congress of American Indians in 1997 recognized her determination to secure transmission of Tewa to succeeding generations of tribal members through both multimedia development (the Tewa Language Project CD-ROM) and traditional storytelling in the language. In 1996 she won recognition as a Living Treasure of New Mexico and in 1998 was one of five New Mexicans honored by the state's governor for excellence and achievement in the arts. Before her last retirement from teaching at San Juan Pueblo she also received many awards for her work at the Pueblo's schools. References to this work appear in the Introduction and in Appendix 3.

We each have met and worked with P'oe Tsá̜wá̜ʔ/Blue Water/Esther Martinez in different ways. Sue-Ellen Jacobs met her in 1972 when she was first conducting ethnohistorical research at San Juan Pueblo. M. Ellien Carroll met her in 1987 while developing and promoting Storytellers International™. Henrietta M. Smith met her during a Storytellers International™ STORYFIESTA™ held at Albuquerque in 1988. In the following sections, we tell our individual stories of meeting Esther Martinez, Blue Water, P'oe Tsá̜wá̜ʔ, or Estefanita Martinez—all names she has used in various publications and other public media.

But first a word about the process of producing this book. M. Ellien Carroll taped most of the stories contained herein. Some were taped in private recording sessions, but most come from the storytelling events that Ellien arranged for Pʼoe Tsą́wą́ʼ. Two stories are from the San Juan Pueblo and University of Washington Tewa Language Project collection. Sue-Ellen recorded those as well as several Coyote stories. It was Ellien's idea to transcribe the stories and make a book of them that would have broad appeal to those in the storytelling business and to individuals interested in Native American oral literature and life histories told through vernacular stories.

Many stories in this collection are allegorical, with animal characters standing in for humans; lessons are to be learned from their successes and mistakes. The language and style of the stories at times are specific to Pueblo locales. At other times a story is metaphorical in reference to problems of discrimination and duties to "Mother Nature," relatives, and others. Sometimes an allegorical tale or a metaphorical example will be found as a story-within-a-story. Some stories are lyrical throughout. Others, such as those surrounding a story-within-a-story, are descriptive, academic, authoritative, facilitative, and always instructional, reflecting Blue Water's love of teaching within and outside of her community.

Originally we were only three editors, Sue-Ellen, Ellien, and Henrietta. First, we needed to find a way to get the tapes transcribed. Sue-Ellen offered to find help for transcription at the University of Washington, and we are fortunate that Tilar Mazzeo, a Ph.D. student in English at the University of Washington, came forward to do that job, which included skillful initial editing. Tilar used transcription and editing conventions most commonly used for representing oral literature in written form. Contractions used in everyday speech such as (in these stories) "I can't go there" become "I can not go there." Most contractions were treated in this fashion.

When transcribing spoken stories, it is common to drop "false starts" as well as "line markers" (such as hmmm, uh, and well) and "asides." Pʼoe Tsą́wą́ʼ's professionalism as a storyteller, whether to a "full house" audience or one person with a videocamera, is apparent on the tapes. She seldom makes false starts and rarely uses line markers. She explained once that when she prepares for a storytelling event she spends a lot of time going over a story in her head and "rehearsing with the hummingbirds, chickens, dogs and cats, whoever will listen" (in either Tewa or English or both) until she has it just right. In September 2002, as we began a new story recording session, P'oe Tsáwą́ʔ said, "Let me say my story to myself in my language, then I'll do it in English."

The practice sessions help P'oe Tsáwą́ʔ manipulate variations in telling and stay on track while reading audience reactions. Practicing with stories lays the foundation for being able to modify one "on the fly" as well as for her different audiences. We have included three versions of "Old Man Bat and the Chickadees" to help demonstrate this process. Esther also works hard to make sure the adjustments are "seamless" so she can avoid false starts, hmmmm, and uh. They are rarely heard on the tapes. Very rare self-correcting incidences (in performance) are not reflected in these stories; we use her corrected version.

Asides are another matter. Sue-Ellen has observed that this is part of community storytelling at San Juan Pueblo. The concept of "literary asides" does not apply to the form of traditional storytelling observed in this community nor in Esther Martinez's service as a consultant in a variety of locales. During 2000 and 2001, for example, Esther and Sue-Ellen (along with our colleague linguist Siri Tuttle) worked with archaeologists on what we called the "land and language project."

We were striving to repatriate or return to San Juan Pueblo the information contained in the writing of John Peabody Harrington.[1] We went through all of the pages in Harrington's *Ethnogeography of the Tewa Indians* pertaining to San Juan Pueblo with the goal of presenting the terms and place names therein in modern Tewa orthography so people using the current writing form could more easily understand Harrington's descriptions and locations. At each language and land session we recorded as many stories about happenings at the places as we did pronunciations, spellings, and meanings of place

---

1. Harrington was a linguist who spent many years studying the various dialects of Upper Rio Grande Tewa, as well as many other Native American languages. He published details of his work in books and journals now long out of print. Harrington published some of his work in collaboration with colleagues and students who worked closely with him on Tewa. This work has value for understanding the ways people at San Juan Pueblo and the other Tewa-speaking pueblos thought about and used language to represent their world during the late 1800s and early 1900s.

names. Storytelling was a central part of processing the information needed for the land research.

The working draft of the book manuscript reflected the order of the tapes as Ellien has labeled her collection, with Sue-Ellen's recorded stories put into the sequence by theme. The second draft was set up sequentially, by complexity of story. Reviewers, however, wanted a different kind of book. They took offense at the fact that we had positioned ourselves at the front of the volume, although they were also very kind. We could still be present, they noted, but should foreground the person we honored. Esther's daughter, Josephine Binford, agreed with the reviewers. Esther liked the previous version but was a good sport about working to make a new version, the present one. By this point the book has had five editors, with Esther Martinez and Josephine Binford taking the lead in the final version.

In presenting the transcriptions, we have indicated where the stories were recorded, whether at an elementary school or before a group of professional healers such as psychiatrists or social workers. On other occasions a story was given at the STORYFIESTA™ in Albuquerque or at special invitational storytelling events such as the Broward County Children's Reading Festival in Fort Lauderdale, Florida in 1992. As you read (and in a few cases listen to) the stories, you get a sense of the way Blue Water pays attention to her audience, makes asides to bring them back to the storyline, or takes them to another aspect of the story that will address their particular circumstance. As part of the "instructional" or pedagogical purpose of this volume, we have included footnotes based on comments P'oe Tsáwą̂ʔ made during our March 2002 meetings to revise the book.

Sue-Ellen's final jobs for the project were to bring the critical comments together, respond to reviewers' questions, type the revised manuscript, and edit the manuscript for technical matters. You have read Josephine Binford's story about her mom. Now we step back so each of the original editors can introduce herself.

Sue-Ellen Jacobs: My story about meeting Esther Martinez begins in 1972 when I was introduced to her by a mutual friend, linguist William (Bill) Leap, now professor of anthropology at American University in Washington, D.C. I was an assistant professor in urban and regional planning at the University of Illinois in Champaign-Urbana and had come to San Juan Pueblo to work on a series of ethnohistorical projects, one involving changing gender roles in Pueblo culture and the other concerned with acquiring stories about life as experienced by elders born before and just after the beginning of the twentieth century.

These stories were to help situate the Pueblo's hope of reclaiming land confirmed as "lost" during the Pueblo Lands Board hearings of the 1920s. In addition to stories of historical use and "grandparent" stories about use in years previous, I was given stories told in Tewa (nominally translated into English) about Pueblo origins and various creations and changes in Pueblo social structure as well as traditional stories that explain why and how the world came to be as it is.

Esther was interested in my efforts and pleased to show me her work on the same topic. As director of bilingual education at the San Juan Pueblo Day School, she was in the process of preparing language learning tools for the children there: curriculum guides, storybooks, and Tewa-English dictionaries. Each form was developed at different levels so children of various ages would incrementally learn to read and write Tewa. At that time, most of the children were still living in homes where most adults spoke the Tewa language along with Spanish and English.

The Bilingual Education Center and program, which had received funding from the National Endowment for the Humanities and support from the Wycliffe Foundation for linguist Randall Speirs's work, became a model for other bilingual education programs throughout the United States.[2] At San Juan Pueblo, community elders were paid for their work in preparing oral and videotapes that Esther and the other members of the Bilingual Program used. One surviving videotape shows the thrilling interactions that occurred as grandmothers and grandfathers, aunts and uncles—respected elders—told stories they had learned from their grandparents to children of various grade levels.

It was a very dynamic and exciting time. Esther and I promised each other that we would share any information we obtained in our

---

2. Speirs's dissertation (1996) was used to create the template for verb inflection found in Martinez, *San Juan Pueblo Tewa Dictionary,* 70–108.

interviews because it pertained to our respective work goals. Little did we know how important that compact would become by the 1990s, when we determined to "bring back language teaching" through a new program, the interactive multimedia Tewa Language Project.

In 1983 the building housing the Bilingual Education Program at the Day School burned to the ground, and all the recorded and written materials Esther and her colleagues had collected and prepared over the previous ten years or so were irretrievably lost. In 1990 I began work to try to return the full range of material I had recorded and otherwise collected since 1972 to the Pueblo. In order to return the stories told in Tewa, I needed help from a linguist, and, of course, I turned to Esther. She agreed to help me get the stories transcribed and translated so they could serve the community's children, who lived in homes where few adults spoke everyday Tewa. I obtained a small grant from the University of Washington's Royalty Research Fund to help pay the cost of our work.

A number of units at the university became interested in our project and over the course of the next eight years provided various levels and kinds of support. The San Juan Pueblo Tribal Council authorized each stage of the work. The Tribal Office and school also sought funding for the portion of work that young people and elders would do as the project grew into an elaborate, interactive multimedia project. We went from "reclamation and repatriation" of stories from elders of the 1970s (and now deceased) to developing learning tools through computer-based technology.

At the outset, as we were learning how to convert analog and text materials to digital sound, video, and text, Esther recorded two stories, "Little Black Ants and Old Man Coyote" and "Old Man Bat and the Chickadees," both included in this volume. Our additional work with stories for the Tewa Language Project will appear in another work. As of this writing, Esther Martinez and Sue-Ellen Jacobs have had a thirty-one-year, very special relationship.

M. Ellien Carroll (Okhúwá Póvi [or Cloud Blossom as Blue Water named me when she saw the sun shining on my white hair]): As I write this tribute to my friend and traveling companion Blue Water (Esther

Martinez), I hear her soft voice as she begins my favorite story with
the Tewa introduction "Owáy wą́hą́ą́-anba yoe." That is the equiva-
lent beginning of Western fairytales: "Once upon a time." The story
"Old Man Bat and the Chickadees" is told to the Pueblo children to
illustrate prejudice and its aftermath.

It has been a great privilege over fifteen years to come to know and
appreciate this humble woman as teacher, communicator, linguist,
historian, and dear friend. Even greater, however, has been the honor
of being able to introduce Blue Water's wisdom, humor, and deep
human insight to the community at large.

I "discovered" Blue Water in 1986 as I browsed in one of my favorite
Albuquerque bookstores. Amid a pile of books carelessly left in a back
corner of the little shop I spotted a small book of stories that had been
translated from Tewa into English for the school children of San Juan
Pueblo. What a gift! At that time my organization, Storytellers Inter-
national™, was in the process of publishing a bilingual magazine, the
Southwest Storytellers Gazette. I contacted Randall Speirs, the editor.
He said Esther Martinez (Blue Water) had translated the stories of her
people and advised me to talk to her. Little did I realize that *she* was
the real gift and would have a profound and lasting effect on my life—
a gift for which I will be forever grateful.

At that time, Blue Water was the director of bilingual education at
the San Juan Day School (now the San Juan Community School). She
invited me to her home for the upcoming San Juan Feast Day. I went,
we met, and, as they say, the rest is history.

During the celebration of this feast day I met her family and many
of the friends and guests who came to her home. It was at this time I
began to learn something of her colorful and adventurous life. Reared
by her grandparents from the age of five, Blue Water speaks wistfully
about the close community where children were never without an
adult within calling distance for guidance, help, or even a snack—
probably hot tortillas to fill an empty tummy.

Following the feast day experience I was overwhelmed by the feeling that as many people as possible must hear Blue Water tell her stories in person. As a strong advocate of family storytelling, I invited Blue
Water to join us for the 1988 STORYFIESTA™ in Albuquerque. This

celebration of the oral tradition became one of the country's largest storytelling festivals. Her acceptance was the beginning of many far-flung storytelling adventures. I later learned that STORYFIESTA™ 1988 was Blue Water's first exposure to non-Native audiences.

Through STORYFIESTA™ and other programs, thousands of children have heard Blue Water's stories. I had—and still have—a deep awareness of the need for children to hear stories related to their family histories. I asked Blue Water if, in addition to her regular presentation, she would be willing to add a covered-dish family meal and program of storytelling to her already long day. She agreed without hesitation. The food provided ranged from tamales wrapped in cornhusks to bologna sandwiches with a juice drink. All were eaten with gusto. Food is always satisfying when prepared with caring hands and consumed in the company of kindred spirits excited and eager to tell and hear stories.

Initial doubt among community leaders about the success of such a venture in an area where people were just "trying to survive" was replaced with amazement and appreciation. Neighbors brought the children of working parents. Grandparents, aunts, uncles, and members of extended families joined in the community storytelling event. Listeners, young and old, laughed and at times became teary. They sat in awe as events in the lives of their loved ones were revealed for the first time. The program was a success. Many children *and* adults benefited from this wondrous fount of history, traditions, and culture. Realizing, however, that adding Family Night to Blue Water's schedule made for a longer work day and more time away from her family, I apologized. Her quiet response was, "Do not be troubled. It is like a vacation for me."

Since Blue Water's first appearance at STORYFIESTA™, invitations have never ceased. We have traveled not only throughout New Mexico but also around the United States to storytelling sites as varied as the people who attended. We went from elegant hotel ballrooms to a ramada of tree branches located only by such instructions as "turn right after the second ash pile." Venues ranged from synagogues to storefront missions and national and international conferences of educators, highway engineers, health care providers, and even the HOGs (Harley Owners Group).

Many organizations' spokespeople were bemused and hesitant when I suggested an elderly, quiet-spoken person rather than a rambunctious, fast-talking entertainer for their jaded audiences. They were willing, however, to trust my judgment and at the end of her presentation were lavish with expressions of gratitude for having been given the gift of her insight and ability to invoke a sense of pride in each person, not only for themselves but also for their communities. As a storyteller, a preserver of history, and a national treasure, Blue Water has given each listener an unforgettable message about the importance of learning, sharing, valuing, and respecting the culture of each of the Creator's children.

Throughout this narrative I have referred to this gracious lady as "Blue Water." That is one of her three names. Each represents a significant part of the history of her people. She is "Estefanita" from the language of the Spanish conquistadors. That name was Americanized to "Esther" at the Indian Boarding School. Born of San Juan Pueblo parents, she was named Blue Water at birth, and that is the name I use in honor of the heritage of which she is deeply proud.

Blue Water has a natural talent for telling her personal stories and those heard from her grandfather. Over the years, although I have heard the stories many times, they are always fresh and interesting. In true oral tradition the heart of the story is always there, but she varies it to suit her listeners. Students of this storytelling art form, writers, and linguists from New Mexico and around the world continue to consult with her. I hope that many more will gain insight into her world through this book.

Henrietta M. Smith (Yellow Mountain [P'i'n Ts'áy]): It was a pleasant fall day in mid-October 1988 when Esther Martinez came into the center where the STORYFIESTA™ was being held. I recognized this beautiful lady with long braids because a sketch of her profile graced the cover of the brochure for that year's fiesta, which was sponsored by Storytellers International™ under the direction of M. Ellien Carroll. When the time came, she quietly shared some of the tales from her Tewa culture. Then she reached into a pocket, pulled out a piece of string, and with remarkably flexible fingers brought a new dimension to the stories by telling them with string. I watched in awe.

Before STORYFIESTA™ was over she said, "My Indian name in English is Blue Water. Perhaps you would like to call me Blue Water." Little did I know how much of a beginning that was to a bond that grows stronger as each year goes by. Over the years I have listened to this wonderful storyteller as she quietly brought to life the characters that are such an important part of her culture—and the lessons embodied in so many of the tales. I heard more than once, with the same respect for her strength and stamina, the recounting of her family's treks across the western part of the country in horse and wagon. And the string. There was always a piece of string. I saw Rabbit go in and out of his house, Coyote get his hair clipped off, and the balloon that became a bunch of bananas. I marveled at Blue Water's patience as she tried to teach me to do these string tales—all to no avail. And yet whenever I asked for another lesson I got it, and with the same grace as if it were the first time.

As we continued to meet at STORYFIESTA™ our friendship grew deeper. Between sessions we talked of many things. To hear her tell me of some of the history and traditions of her people was like sitting at the feet of a master storyteller and learning something new at each meeting.

In 1992 we shared an unforgettable time in Florida. M. Ellien Carroll brought Blue Water to the Children's Reading Festival sponsored by the Broward County Public Library System. This time Blue Water was the featured teller, bringing to old and young stories of her Tewa childhood, the familiar tales of Rabbit and Coyote, and, of course, stories with the ever-present piece of string. There was no end to the questions from the audience about her life, her Native dress, her education, and much more. When the "work" part of the visit was over we went to the beach, and I watched with quiet appreciation Blue Water's love and respect for the things of nature. She took back to her Pueblo a bit of Florida sand, sea shells, a few leaves from a sea grape tree, and a tiny feather dropped by a tern—items that one who lives there takes for granted.

Our friendship was further cemented when I was invited to come to the Pueblo and join her family at the time of the Deer Dance Festival. I witnessed Blue Water, the revered elder, dressing her grandsons for the dance, arranging their clothes, and painting their faces for the traditional ceremony. I witnessed her grandchildren, at the end of the day, sitting at her feet, crouching on each side of her, or leaning over her shoulder from the back of the couch, listening to the stories they have probably heard many times before. The Pueblo storyteller doll was alive!

I know that our friendship will last forever with this one more crowning act of togetherness. On a quiet evening, Blue Water said, "I want to give you your Indian name." Thank you, Blue Water, for all the history, the joy and love that has come from knowing you.

GLOSSARY OF TEWA TERMS

Ahkon Póvi: Prairie Flower (proper name)
atole (Spanish): a gruel or drink made from blue cornmeal; boiled blue cornmeal; ągän (Tewa)

buwá: bread, also known as piki bread; thin blue cornmeal bread

Chimayo: a town in New Mexico (see Tsimayoe)

e'nú: a teenaged boy
enúkáy: a little boy

haheyinḍa'mannamu: this is how long the story is (comparable to "the end")

khâaveh: the number eight
khapo: a rose
ko'êe'ây: little chickadees
kó'ôe (aunt): term used to show respect for women who may or may not be related to the speaker
khų́ų: corn
Khų́ų Ko P'oé: the month of Corn Planting

nangeh: floor
naví p'ôe'ą́ą̈: my life's path
núnú'aa: Native dress

Ohkay Owînge: San Juan Pueblo (also *Ohkay Owêengeh* and *Ohkay Owîngeh*)

ók'uḍa: the grinding stone

Okhúwá Póvi: Cloud Blossom (proper name)

owáy wậhậä-anba yoe: once upon a time

paa: fish

p'ậạnú: the number five

pedapusabe: stink bug

pehtsiye: storytelling

Pehtsiye-ây: Little Tewa Stories

Pénít'aa E'nú: Skeleton Boy (proper name)

piñons: small, shelled pine nuts about the size of a sunflower seed

P'ín Ts'áy: Yellow Mountain (proper name)

poe: pumpkin

póe: moon

poeyeh: the number three

p'oe: water

P'oe Tsậwậ': Blue Water (proper name)

p'oe sậ'wậ: water squirrel

p'ôe: road

P'ósewhâa Sedó: Old Man Coyote (proper name)

Pókhávi E'nú: Broken Gourd Boy (proper name)

posole: cornmeal stew

P'osuwäge: Pojoaque Pueblo in New Mexico ("water drinking place")

sahkéwe: thick cornmeal mush

sa'yâa: grandmother

sengithamu: good morning (greeting)

sí: the number six

Síphêe Sedó: Old Man Bat (proper name)

thehtáy: grandfather

titíḍí: water spider

tsą́wą́ʔ: the color blue

tą̈: the number ten

Tsimayoe (Chimayo): a town in New Mexico (*tsi* means "walking," *mayoe* means "being tired")

tsį́ʔwą́nuʔây: little black ants

tséh: the number seven

tsídé: bird

vegas (Spanish): exposed ceiling beams made from tree trunks; *tephé* (Tewa)

wąą: wind

wée tsiʔtsi: squeak

whą̈ä: wild weeds

whą̈änu: the number nine

whǫʔphą̈ʔ: mattress or bedding

wíʔ: the number one

wíyeh: the number two

wówátsi: life

yôenu: the number four

APPENDIX 1: EXAMPLES OF AUDIENCES' QUESTIONS AND MY ANSWERS

TRADITIONAL SEASONAL GAMES

You know when you talked about different seasons, different games and the seasons? What kinds of games did you play in the summer, and what kind in the winter?

Winter games were jacks for girls and tops for boys. Usually the winter games would go on until almost spring begins. The elders of the village come to every house and tell the parents. In my case, it was a grandmother and grandfather. They tell them, "Tell the children to put away their jacks, put away their tops. We are going into warmer weather."

Spring is when they have the shinny games. Do you know what shinny games are? See, they have curved sticks. They go way curvy. That is a girl's stick, when it is real curvy and with a long handle. You get it and hit the ball. And you have sides. Somebody on the other side will try to hit it on this side. We play in the village. And if they can take it to the last house on the other side, they win. But if we do not let them take it over there and if we can bring the ball on this side, to the house that is built on this side, then we win. And the boys' sticks are just barely curved because they hit theirs hard, and they can make it go up higher or faster. Shinny games. And that starts when they start planting, about in March.

They have the seed game first. All the men go out and have a seed game. They take the seed game out to the fields. It is called seed game because the ball is filled with seeds. Everybody from the village takes seeds to the Summer Chief's house. He is the one that makes the ball. He paints it yellow because yellow is their color—like the sun. So, the

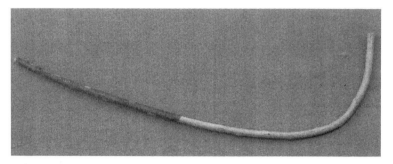

Figure 32. San Juan Pueblo shinny stick, 1997. (Sue-Ellen Jacobs)

boys will be waiting with their shinny sticks on the other side, and he throws it over. He is on this side of the row of houses, and he will throw it on the other side. When they get it, they try to take it to their homes.

The women are waiting with goodies. They might have brought apples, and they might have made fry bread. Now there is candy and stuff like that. But when I was growing up it was just fry bread. The only kind of fruit that they had was apples. Remember, I told you that they hang them up in the ceiling? There is a kind of apple that lasts all winter long. They are just little ones. They are golden, with red on one side. They tie the tails with a string, and then there is the vegas [exposed ceiling beams made from tree trunks]. And in between the vegas they put the sticks—like a toothpick. They did not have toothpicks, but they make little sticks to tie the fruit on. This takes a lot of patience. They do that for children. They stick it up there. And when there is a child who comes to visit them, it is like picking an apple off a tree. They will get it down and give it to the child. If they still have apples, they will throw them out to the ball players along with fry bread and tamales or whatever else they might have.

And they play until the ball busts. If it does not bust today, they will take it out tomorrow again. And the boys who have fields [to be planted] on that side will try to take it that way. And there are some who have their fields over on this other side, they will take it that way. Wherever it busts is where they quit. But they gather the seed that is in the ball and take it home and mix it with whatever seed they are going to plant. That is the seed game.

And from then on it is shinny games. The young boys challenge the married men. The single boys challenge the married men. And the winner will ask for a dance. So the losers will have to dance for them. If it is the young boys who lost, they are the ones who dance, and then the married men will have to get something ready to eat, to feed them. Like a feast. And they feed the dancers. So nobody really loses. They dance, and then the other folks feed them. Which means the married men get their wives to cook. And they feed them. And the single boys, if they need women partners, they get the single girls to dance along with them. So it is just a fun thing all the time. So that is spring.

And then summertime. Summertime is hunting, mostly hunting. There are the bows and arrows, and they go hunting. I do not think we have had any kids who would be a good shot with a bow and an arrow to bring home a rabbit to eat. But they aim at whatever they have, maybe a corn stalk. Or they put out something—cardboard—and aim at that.

And then, there is always swimming in the river. The bigger ones have their own place for swimming because they know how to swim. And then the smaller ones are taken with the big brothers to their place of swimming, where they can just play in the sand and build mud houses. And that is summertime.

In the autumn is when they make the bows and arrows, and they have the shooting contest. They try to see whose arrow will fly the farthest. Because I have my little brother to take care of, I had learned how to play boys' games. I learned how to shoot a bow and arrow, and I learned how to make the bows. I used to make them for him. And I learned how to play marbles with the big boys and win enough marbles to share with my brother. But he has to come across with something!

One time, my grandmother made us pottery. We ate out of pottery. We did not have store-bought dishes. Always pottery. Pottery to eat out of. And she had pottery pots to cook from and big pots like that to store her seeds in. They were buried against the wall in the ground, so she put a board covering on the top of the opening of the pottery. This is filled up with seeds and then a cover. Then she plasters over that with mud.

We have a mud floor. We did not have floors like this [points to

Figure 33. Hands of a San Juan Pueblo potter, 1978. (Sue-Ellen Jacobs)

the tile floor at the school]. It was always a mud floor. The woman of the house had to be the one to keep that floor looking nice. My grandmother said that we were like horses, my little brother and I. We wore shoes that had a heel, and it would wear out the floor. They wore moccasins, and that is just like walking barefoot. So there were games.

CHANGES IN PUEBLO LIFE

From the time when you moved to San Juan Pueblo to now there have been a lot of changes. What do you see as the biggest change from the time you were a little girl to now?[1]

Well, there are a lot of changes that have taken place. One thing is that the language is going, and it is going fast. Another thing, we do

---

1. "Changes in Pueblo Life." Tape 4, told at STORYFIESTA™, 1997. Recorded by M. Ellien Carroll. Transcribed and edited by Tilar Mazzeo; edited by Sue-Ellen Jacobs, Henrietta M. Smith, and M. Ellien Carroll.

not live in the village in the way we used to. Long ago, when a family lived there, every door in the village had a family living there; now we have about four families living in the plaza where I used to live. There are a lot of vacant houses, and there are a lot of houses that have been knocked down and have never been rebuilt.

Another change is that, with those houses closed up, now the young people are living in HUD houses, away from the village, so that they do not stay close together. They do not share the work or share the food the way it was shared before—you know, work and food and caring for one another.

We had our elderly people living in their own little homes. They did not have to leave their houses. People would go and gather wood. Somebody would be washing clothes, and they would go to the elders' homes and pick up their laundry and wash it, dry it. In those days, you did not iron it; you would shake them so that the wind irons them, then fold it up and take it back to them. Somebody would come and sweep their house, another one would cook more than enough so that they could take some to the seniors. Seniors had it made; just like the senior citizens programs they have now, it was just like that. We took care of them, the elders, with those things, so that they do not have to leave their homes.

All the changes that you mention seem to be changes for the worse. Are there any changes for the better?

Well the kiva language is still intact, and that is good. The kiva language is a real old language. It is a different, a special language. It is not an everyday language. It is not language that is used in the home. It is language that is taught to young boys by men only. I just found out that my boys were talking women's language because I cared for them. I took care of them and talked to them the way I spoke the language. One of my boys is just now learning how to talk the kiva language. And that is interesting because it is a real old language, that is the language they use in saying prayers.

Do almost all of the young people still go through an initiation and do they participate . . .

Yes, they still go through initiation, they still go through initiation. We have a Summer side and a Winter side. The Winter side is pretty active. On the Summer side, we had two leaders who had very negative attitudes. They were leaders, but they had negative attitudes. There were some young boys who wanted to join the elders so that they can carry on the jobs of the men on their side, but I guess the two leaders thought they were going to live forever. They said no. So that is the only thing that is bad. On the Winter side they are still pretty active.

Women also? The women are also still going through initiation?

Yes, the young boys and the young women all get initiated; it depends. If they belong to the Winter side, they get initiated to the Winter clan, and for the Summer people there is Summer side. But they are slower at doing it, sometimes they skip a year.

Does it depend on when they are born?

No. From way back, when the people were coming to the pueblo, they traveled in two groups. The Winter people came over the mountains. They did the hunting, they are the hunters. And the Summer people came through the valleys, and they are the takers. They take berries, they take whatever greens they can get for eating. Then, after traveling so many days, they all came together. Winter people share their meat with the Summer people, and the Summer people share whatever they have gathered in the way of berries and greens with the Winter people. So they shared. That is how the Winter people came about; they were hunters coming over the mountains. And the Summer people traveled below.

People who are descended from them, their children and the children's children, are they still Winter people and Summer people?

Yes, unless a Winter woman marries a Summer man. Then she automatically is a Summer person, and her children will be Summer people. Unless there is a son that might want to stay with the Winter people. A grandmother or an elderly person might want to have one of the grandkids belong to the Summer side. I have a son who stayed with my mother. My mother asked for a boy to go with her to the kiva and accompany her wherever she had to go. So I let her keep one of my boys. He is a Winter man, the only Winter man in the family. The rest of them are Summer people. But he forgets, now and then, where to stand when he goes to the kiva, when he is going to dance. The Summer people have their own clay, well not clay, it is a slip that they put on their dancers. It is a slip that they get from the river bed. It is black, very black, and they put it on their faces. The Winter people wear red. So, sometimes my son comes home painted red. He is a Winter person, not a Summer man when he has that red on; and then, if you get him in the right place when he has that black on, he is a Summer man. So he dances either as a Winter or Summer, but he is a Winter man.

There is the possibility that all our roofs are connected to each other, right? Could not the whole part of the pueblo collapse if people do not hold up their end?

Yes, it will, in fact. The place that we had is no longer there, where I grew up. Somebody starting taking the rafters, and the roof is not there any more. The walls were still there; but when they want adobes, they just help themselves to our building. But there were five families in that part. I do not know how many are on the other side. There are more on the other side. But their houses are passed onto the children, and if the children do not take care of the houses, then they fall.

If the elders want a house to remain, can they ask people to come and help?

They will fix them.

Did anyone come back, did anyone related to the elders come back and build it back up?

It seems like now the younger ones want houses the way you have your houses. They do not want to be bothered with repairing of the floors and the walls. They have been away from the village. The dances are still done in the village. There is a place behind a church where it is called "the heart of the pueblo." It is still there. When they have the Harvest Dance in the fall, all the dancers who come with the food for the Harvest Dance, they will break a whole watermelon right where the heart of the village is, and then they dance along there.

Figure 34. Aerial view of San Juan Pueblo homes, a chapel, church, and more, 1975. (John D. Jacobs)

Do you have dates?
    On the twenty-fourth of June.

Do a lot of people come?
    Yes. A lot of people come. We prepare a lot of food. Friends come eat with their friends. They are always welcome. It does not matter whether you are invited or not. When you have a friend from the village, you just go, and you know you are going to get food to eat. It is nice. And that is a day when you can see your friends. Sometimes you see your friends in the village and you tell them to come, and if they are too busy dancing or doing something else, then they do not come. But we always have a lot of stuff.

Do you go to anybody else's feast?
    Oh yes, I go to Santa Clara, and I go to the other villages. That is a day when you do not take your lunch; you go just the way you are, you know you are going to get something to eat.

APPENDIX 2: TRADITIONAL STORYTELLING AT SAN JUAN PUEBLO

Sue-Ellen Jacobs with Esther Martinez (P'oe Tsā́wā́ʔ)

At San Juan Pueblo, New Mexico, storytelling serves both sacred and secular purposes. Sacred storytelling is usually performed by men in the kivas as part of ceremonial preparation, initiation of the young, and other matters requiring private communication concerning religious matters. None of the kiva stories are ever told in public. Both women and men tell secular stories in various public settings. Public storytelling used to be done only in the winter, but by the 1990s traditional storytellers could be found telling many different types of stories throughout the year in schools, at health and other types of conferences, intertribal gatherings, and storytelling festivals.

San Juan Pueblo people who are "traveling" storytellers include Clarence Cata, Peter Garcia, and Esther Martinez, who is usually booked by her Tewa name, P'oe Tsā́wā́ʔ (Blue Water). At the senior center, where people gather for social and recreational time on the reservation, some elders recount stories of their lives as well as stories they heard while growing up from grandparents and parents. This kind of storytelling is part of everyday life for many children and adults at San Juan Pueblo. There are some homes where "formal" storytelling is not done, yet even in these homes parents will tell stories about what happened to them at work during the day or when they went on a trip. In other words, storytelling is a central part of life, even when it seems that traditional stories are not being told.

When it is time for the community to prepare for a ceremonial event, generally referred to as "dances," people will be told that a ceremony is to take place on a certain day. About a week before that day,

---

This essay is based in large part on our article "Traditional Storytelling at San Juan Pueblo."

the elders explain to everyone who comes to practice how the ceremony came to be, why it is being done, what it means, and how everyone is supposed to think about the ceremony as well as behave during it. The explanations are told in the form of stories, some long, some quite short. The point is to get everyone ready spiritually and physically for the full day of ceremonial dance. Some of the dances are stories, but the songs that accompany them are always stories. These song stories may describe events in nature, relationships between people and the spiritual world, some aspect of Pueblo history, or other events. There is no age limit for participation in these ceremonial events.

"EACH CHILD IS ITS OWN STORY"

In preparation for a ceremonial event such as getting ready for the 1996 Yellow Corn Dance, children tell stories about their own efforts to acquire the special clothing and other items they must wear, about being afraid of going out to dance the actual performance of the ceremony in public for the first time, and how good they feel about participating in a communitywide event of such importance. The elders always tell the children how much they appreciate their performances.

In the 1970s a number of stories were recorded from elders who were raised in traditional Tewa storytelling practices. This was an important community project because traditional storytelling was on the wane. As in other communities, television and other imported media distracted family and larger community audiences away from local stories. So, in an effort to preserve them, "old" stories were collected from elders by various family members, friends, and anthropologists and by Esther Martinez, the founder and director of the Bilingual Program at the San Juan Pueblo Community School, formerly San Juan Pueblo Day School, under direction of the Bureau of Indian Affairs.

Although the majority of the stories were recorded on audiotape, some were recorded on videotape. These recordings were to form the core of a cultural preservation program, but, sadly, most were destroyed in a cataclysmic fire at the school in 1983. Now we are involved in an effort to reclaim and restore stories collected by others during that period and subsequently. At this time [1996] we are working with forty stories, some of which have their origins in the late 1800s, with language and culture preservation and restoration goals in mind. Readers who are interested in Tewa stories collected in the early 1900s will want to read Elsie Clews Parsons, *Tewa Tales* (1994 [1926]).

When P'oe Tsáwą́ʔ tells stories to children at the school, the teachers prepare the children by having them sit in a circle, often on the floor, while she sits on a chair. Most of her stories are told in English even though they are based on original Tewa stories. Her stories cover those that are best suited for teaching children about nature, solving personal problems (including peer problems), the history of the everyday community life in years past, and aspects of contemporary life. When telling stories to a large audience of adults—for example, telling stories intended for healing to people attending health conferences—Blue Water usually stands. These stories include those having to do with losing family members, disappointments, sorrow, loneliness, happiness, and overcoming or otherwise taking care of other forms of stress. Such stories are similar to those told in Tewa by people at the Pueblo to help with healing.

Audience response varies according to the type, style, context, and function of the story being told. Ceremonial events are not performed for an audience, yet people from the Pueblo and outsiders gather to witness the performance. They become an audience in the theatrical sense of the word, but they are not expected to respond audibly unless invited to do so by the dancers, singers, leaders, or other officials. The job of the audience generally is to be silent and respectful; applauding is considered inappropriate. A similar ambiance (mood, behavior, environment) is expected when a storyteller commences and gives the story, whether to small children, young people, or adults. The job of the audience again is to be silent and respectful unless invited to answer a question. When a story is completed, the audience may ask questions, may verbally thank the storyteller, or may applaud in some circumstances. Depending on the situation, a storyteller may dress in everyday clothes or may dress in traditional clothing. When Blue Water (Esther Martinez) goes to tell stories in non-Native environments she wears formal traditional clothing such as is worn by women during ceremonial dances or on feast days. She does so to give her audiences the additional gift of seeing her special clothing. When stories are to be told at the school or other places in the Pueblo, she dresses in her everyday clothes.

In our work together we are trying to build a bridge from the past to the future using the cultural traditions we each have been given. Because storytelling has been such an integral part of these traditions, we are exploring the use of various visual and other means to convey a sense of old-fashioned storytelling through the medium that seems to enchant the present generation: computer technology. We do not expect, however, that this new technology will replace the power and wonder children of all ages experience when a storyteller gives a story to an audience in person.

APPENDIX 3: RÉSUMÉ OF ESTHER MARTINEZ

Esther Martinez
(names used as storyteller: P'oe Tsáwą̌', Blue Water, and Estefanita Martinez)

PROFESSIONAL EXPERIENCE

1989–present   Traditional storyteller for National Park Service, public and private schools, and professional organizations such as the National Association of Psychiatrists using storytelling for healing. Tewa-language consultation to various linguists, public and private schools, including the University of California, Crow Canyon Archaeological Research Center, University of New Mexico, University of Washington, Santa Clara Pueblo School, Ohkay Owîngéh School, Tesuque Public School, and more.

1995–98   Co-director, Tewa Language Project, San Juan Pueblo, N.M.

1985–89   Tewa language consultant to San Juan Pueblo Day School and San Juan Pueblo Public School.

1984   Instructor, Summer Institute of Linguistics for Native Americans, University of New Mexico, Santa Fe campus.

1978–85   Bilingual Education Program director and teacher, San Juan Pueblo Day School.

Many dates are approximate.

1974–78   Tewa language teacher, kindergarten through sixth grade, San Juan Pueblo Elementary School.

various years   Worked at Santa Fe Indian Hospital, Dulce Jicarilla Apache Hospital, and at various locales in Los Alamos.

HONORS AND AWARDS

1999   Indigenous Language Institute Award for "Those Who Make a Difference."

1998   New Mexico Arts Commission Governor's Award for Excellence and Achievement in the Arts.

1997   Indian Education Award for Teacher of the Year from the National Council of American Indians, Woman of the Year Award.

1996   Living Treasure Award from state of New Mexico.

1995, 1996   Co-recipient of two Chamisza Foundation Awards for Tewa Language Project at San Juan Pueblo.

1992   National Association for Bilingual Education, Pioneer Award.

1980s   Co-recipient of multiple National Institute of Education awards for bilingual education programs at San Juan Pueblo Day School and for publication of bilingual education material.

PUBLICATIONS

1997–2000   Translations of Tewa-language text materials for Tewa Language Project CD-ROM, multiple versions. Audio recordings of Tewa and English words for the full language database. Two videotaped stories recorded, transcribed, and translated on the CD-ROM "Stories" application.

1999   "Traditional Story Telling at San Juan Pueblo" (with Sue-Ellen Jacobs). In *Traditional Storytelling*

Today: An International Encyclopedia, edited by Margaret Read MacDonald, 381–82. Chicago: Fitzroy Dearborn.

1998   "Multimedia Technology in Language and Culture Restoration Efforts at San Juan Pueblo: A Brief History of the Development of the Tewa Language Project," *Wicazo Sa Review* 13(2): 45–58 (with Sue-Ellen Jacobs and Siri Tuttle).

1978–98   Various booklets, jointly written papers, and books written in collaboration with Bilingual Program at San Juan Pueblo, with linguists and anthropologists at various universities: William Leap at American University, Washington, D.C., Sue-Ellen Jacobs at the University of Washington, Seattle, and Siri Tuttle at University of California, Los Angeles. Sole author of several Tewa and bilingual Tewa-English storybooks (some of which are listed below).

1992   *The Naughty Little Rabbit and Old Man Coyote.* Chicago: Children's Press, (o.p.).

1989   *Tewa Language Curriculum Guide, Level Three* (contributor). San Juan Pueblo Bilingual Program.

1984   *Tewa Language Curriculum Guide, Level Two* (compiler and editor). San Juan Pueblo Bilingual Program.

1984   *Tewa Tᵾᵾkannin Tą'nin.* Edited by Esther Martinez (contributing author), Randall H. Speirs, and Ann Speirs. San Juan Pueblo Bilingual Program.

1983   *Tewa Language Curriculum Guide, Level One* (compiler and editor). San Juan Pueblo Bilingual Program.

1982   *San Juan Pueblo Tewa Dictionary* (compiler and co-editor, with Randall H. Speirs and members of the San Juan Pueblo Bilingual Program).

EDUCATIONAL BACKGROUND

1982	University of New Mexico, Santa Fe branch. Summer Institute of Linguistics for Native Americans (SILNA), Part 2.
1980	University of New Mexico, Albuquerque, Summer Institute of Linguistics for Native Americans (SILNA), Part 1.
1978–84	University of New Mexico, Albuquerque campus, Teacher Training Program.
1974	Summer Institute of Linguistics, North Dakota.
1952	Santa Fe Indian Hospital, nurse's aide training.
1931	Albuquerque Indian School, high school diploma.

A NOTE ABOUT THE AUDIO FILES "STORIES FROM SAN JUAN PUEBLO"

The audio files were captured and edited by Sue-Ellen Jacobs and Charles Hiestand using "Gold Wave" on a Compaq Presario 1500T using analog cassette tape recordings made by Ellien Carroll and Sue-Ellen Jacobs of Esther Martinez's original storytelling sessions. The captured files were processed and mastered by Larri Sims and Charles Hiestand at Creative Art Studios in Seattle, Washington, using a Macintosh G4 and ProTools Digi001 version.

The audio files (available at https://www.press.uillinois.edu/books/ martinez/my_life/) contain seven stories, some matching exactly the text version of the story published in this book, and others that are a slightly different version told in a different setting than noted in the text.

Track No. 1: "Little Black Ants and Coyote" (8:22), compare to "Little Black Ants and Old Man Coyote" (pp. 93–97).

Track No. 2: "Lazy Coyote and Mrs. Turkey" (5:13), compare to "Lazy Coyote and Mrs. Turkey" (pp. 102–3).

Track No. 3: "Grandmother Spider, Coyote, and the Stars" (7:06), identical to text version (pp. 105–6).

Track No. 4: "Mr. Coyote's Feast" (7:46), identical to text version (pp. 107–10).

Track No. 5: "The Deer Story" (19:22), compare to "The Deer Story" (pp. 111–17).

Track No. 6: "Old Man Bat and the Chickadees" (9:04), identical to text version one (pp. 118–24).

Track No. 7: "Two White Corn Maidens and Gourd Boy" (8:22), identical to text version one (pp. 136–39).

As indicated in the Epilogue (pp. 151–61), storytellers do not always tell a story the same way. Different audiences, different settings, and varying amounts of time determine whether a story is told in full form or whether parts are left out to accommodate a given session. Some stories are from performances before either large or small audiences; others were told in private recording sessions for purposes of improving audio quality. Further information can be found in the footnote for each story.

SOURCES CITED

Jacobs, Sue-Ellen, and Esther Martinez. 1998. "Multimedia Technology in Language and Culture Restoration Efforts at San Juan Pueblo: A Brief History of the Development of the Tewa Language Project." *Wicazo Sa Review* 13(2): 45–58.

———. 1999. "Traditional Storytelling at San Juan Pueblo." In *Traditional Storytelling Today: An International Encyclopedia,* ed. Margaret Read MacDonald, 381–82. Chicago: Fitzroy Dearborn.

Martinez, Estefanita. 1992. *The Naughty Little Rabbit and Old Man Coyote: A Tewa Story from San Juan Pueblo.* Chicago: Children's Press.

Martinez, Esther. 1983. *San Juan Pueblo Tewa Dictionary.* San Juan Pueblo Bilingual Program.

Parsons, Elsie Clews. 1926. *Tewa Tales.* American Folk-Lore Society Memoir 19. Reprint 1994 with a new foreword by Barbara Babcock. Tucson: University of Arizona Press.

———. 1929. *The Social Organization of the Tewa of New Mexico.* American Anthropological Association Memoir 36:1–309.

Speirs, Randall. 1966. "Some Aspects of the Structure of Rio Grande Tewa." Ph.D. diss., SUNY at Buffalo.

ADDITIONAL READINGS

Applegate, Frank G. 1929. *Indian Stories from the Pueblos.* Philadelphia: J. B. Lippincott. Reprint 1988. Glorieta, N.M.: Rio Grande Press.

Evers, Larry, and Barre Toelken. 1998. "Introduction: Collaboration in the Translation and Interpretation of Native American Oral Traditions." *Oral Tradition* (special issue on Native American oral traditions: collaboration and interpretation) 13(1): 1–12.

Tyler, Hamilton A. 1964. *Pueblo Gods and Myths.* Norman: University of Oklahoma Press.

———. 1975. *Pueblo Animals and Myths.* Norman: University of Oklahoma Press.

Vallo, Lawrence Jonathon. 1987. *Tales of a Pueblo Boy.* Santa Fe, N.M.: Sunstone Press.

LINGUISTIC, ETHNOGRAPHIC, ENVIRONMENTAL, AND NATURAL HISTORY SOURCES

Harrington, John Peabody. 1916. "The Ethnogeography of the Tewa Indians." In *Twenty-ninth Annual Report of the Bureau of American Ethnology to the Secretary of the Smithsonian Institution, 1907–1908,* 29–636. Washington: Government Printing Office.

———. 1919. "Meanings of Old Tewa Indian Placenames around Santa Fe." In *El Palacio,* 78–83.

———. Robbins, Wilfred William, John Peabody Harrington, and Barbara Freire-Marreco. 1916. *Ethnobotany of the Tewa Indians.* Smithsonian Institution Bureau of American Ethnology Bulletin 55. Washington: Government Printing Office.

ESTHER MARTINEZ is an enrolled tribal member of San Juan Pueblo, New Mexico. A retired teacher of Tewa language and culture, she has become well-known for her gift of storytelling in her native language, Tewa, and in English. She has won numerous awards, including the New Mexico Governor's Award for Excellence and Achievement in the Arts, and recognition as a "Living Treasure of New Mexico" in 1998. She is the principal author of the San Juan Pueblo *Tewa Language Dictionary* and numerous bilingual storybooks and curricula guides.

SUE-ELLEN JACOBS is a professor of women studies, adjunct professor of anthropology, and adjunct professor of music at the University of Washington in Seattle. She has worked on various applied anthropology projects with San Juan Pueblo since 1972, and with Esther Martinez and others completed the multimedia, three CD-ROM applications for the San Juan Pueblo Tewa Language Project in 2000. She has numerous publications based on her work as an anthropologist in this and other communities.

JOSEPHINE BINFORD is one of Esther Martinez's three daughters. A public health nurse who practices out of the Santa Fe Indian Health Service Unit, she specializes in gerontology. She has returned to San Juan Pueblo after many years in other parts of the country in order to take part in traditional Pueblo life, care for her mother, and help her mother participate in storytelling events.

M. ELLIEN CARROLL grew up on a farm in southern Michigan. She attended her first university class at age thirty-eight and, while rearing three children, graduated several years later with an MLS. She is the founder of Storytellers International™.

HENRIETTA M. SMITH, a native New Yorker, is professor emerita with the School of Library and Information Science at the University of South Florida in Tampa, where a residency has been established in her name at the University Library. Her storytelling skills were encouraged and honed by Augusta Baker in the New York Public Library system, and she participated in the programs of Storytellers International™ for eleven years.

TILAR MAZZEO received her Ph.D. in English from the University of Washington and is an assistant professor of English at the University of Wisconsin at Oshkosh, with particular interest in women's studies and environmental studies.

TESSIE NARANJO is an enrolled member of Santa Clara Pueblo and holds a Ph.D. in sociology from the University of New Mexico. She has undertaken numerous research projects for her tribe, including serving on the Santa Clara Pueblo language committee. She has worked as a consultant for national, state, and local museums as well as for various private archaeological organizations. She was chair of the review committee implementing aspects of the Native American Graves Protection and Repatriation Act and is vice president of the board of the Indigenous Languages Institute. She has numerous publications directly related to her research in the social history of her tribe and her work with language preservation and teaching.

INDEX

The University of Illinois Press
is a founding member of the
Association of American University Presses.

_____

University of Illinois Press
1325 South Oak Street
Champaign, IL 61820-6903
www.press.uillinois.edu